A NEW LIGHT
ON
ANGELS

A NEW LIGHT
ON
ANGELS

© Diana Cooper 1996, 2009

The right of Diana Cooper to be identified as the author
of this work has been asserted by her in accordance with the
Copyright, Designs and Patents Act 1998.

Includes material from *A Little Light on Angels*
first published in 1996 by Findhorn Press.
Published in 2009 by Findhorn Press, Scotland

ISBN 978-1-84409-166-9

Edited by Michael Hawkins
Cover, interior design and illustrations by Damian Keenan
Printed and bound in the European Union

3 4 5 6 7 8 9 10 11 12 14 13 12

Published by
Findhorn Press
305a The Park, Findhorn
Forres IV36 3TE
Scotland, UK

Telephone
+44-(0)1309-690582
Fax
+44-(0)131-777-2177

info@findhornpress.com
www.findhornpress.com

A NEW LIGHT
ON
ANGELS

DIANA COOPER

FINDHORN PRESS

Contents

Contents

To the angels

with love

and thanks

My Introduction To Angels

Angels have been part of my life for so long that it is hard to remember a time when I did not sense their presence and know that they would help me.

But I came from a non spiritual, non religious background, with parents who were totally sceptical of anything psychic or intangible. They considered religion to be a crutch and psychic phenomena to be imagination or chicanery. So I never really considered the possibility of angels or dimensions beyond the visible world. Looking back I think my intuitive knowing of a spiritual world was in conflict with the information I was fed. This was why I was forced to have such a difficult wake up call.

In my early forties I had lived overseas for some years. Back in the UK I knew no one and my children were in boarding school. My marriage was in ruins and my self esteem and confidence were negligible. My mind was full of dark imaginings for I could see no light ahead. In this black despair I threw myself into a chair and demanded, 'If there is anything out there, show me and you've got one hour.' (I was going out an hour later).

That was when an angel, a golden being of light, appeared and took my spirit on a journey. Several times the angel took me up to a hill top and pushed me. I fell and was always held by the light. Once I was strapped into a rocket and propelled forward very fast, until suddenly everything turned to light. Then we moved on to the most important part of the experience for me. The angel and I flew together, side by side, over a hall full of people who had rainbow auras, so I knew they were spiritually evolved.

I asked the angel if I was down there in the audience and it replied, 'No you are on the platform.' I saw that on the platform were three transparent beings with rays of light flowing through and from them. The angel communicated that I was to be a teacher. Instantly I knew that I had much work ahead of me to purify my energy fields. When the angel returned me to my body it was exactly one hour later and I had received or remembered much cosmic information.

I knew that I had been given a profound and important experience but I was not quite sure what to do with it, so I wrote it down and waited. A few days after the angel visit I went to the library where a book on healing fell off the shelf. I devoured the words for I passionately wanted to help people. I recalled an occasion when I was travelling on a ferry which broke down. For five hours the boat was adrift in the English Channel. I was sitting next to a very loquacious lady who had given up smoking and then lost weight through hypnosis. I was fascinated and asked question after question. It stirred my interest in the importance of hypnotherapy.

Soon after the angel experience I decided to train to be a hypno-therapist and healer. My then husband had taken away my cheque book so I found a series of menial jobs to pay for the training. On the first day of the course he stood over me with arms akimbo forbidding me to do such an 'insane' thing but I managed to do it anyway.

During the first weekend I was a guinea pig for the teacher. She gave me basic hypnosis for release of stress and confidence building. It was wonderful! I returned home feeling safe and confident for the first time in years. All my husband's jibes and taunts slid off my aura without affecting me. At last I found the strength to get out of my marriage, move house and set up in practice.

Over the next ten years my life changed completely. I moved onto a spiritual path, though not a religious one, for although I accept that all religions are pathways up the spiritual mountain I do not belong to one. At the top of the mountain there is oneness and it is only lower down that the paths diverge and people no longer understand or accept each other.

Although I was aware from time to time of angels helping me with my clients, I communicated first and foremost with my spirit guides. In these years I had many psychic and spiritual experiences. I wanted to meet the spirit guide who was helping me at that time. So I sat in meditation every evening and visualised myself walking up the spiritual mountain, then sitting at the brow waiting for my guide to connect. Eventually Bartholomew entered my life. I had to wait another ten years before I met Kumeka, my current guide.

Then one summer evening I was lying in the bath, soaking in the soft warmth of the bubbly water and contemplating my forthcoming

Healing and Psychic Development class. I requested spiritual guidance, asking, "What is this class about?" Suddenly a golden voice, or more precisely a powerful clear thought in my head said, "You are to introduce them to healing with angels."

Totally startled I exclaimed, "But I don't know anything about healing with angels."

The voice responded, "Yes, you do. It's just not conscious yet."

"Oh," I said, "But I can't do that on the first class of the new term. Some of them haven't been before."

The answer was straightforward: "Who's running the class — your ego or your higher guidance?"

I took the point and asked, "Well, what's the difference between healing with guides, spiritual healing and angelic healing?"

The voice said, "Angels will lift you both to God." I presumed this meant both the healer and the person being healed. Without pause the voice continued, "You need a solid golden space to invite the angels into. Make it."

Stunned, I jumped out of the bath and, wrapped in a towel sat on the bed. Three angels stood in front of me and gave me information. I wrote it all down and it became the basis for the original version of this book, *A Little Light on Angels*. I also assumed any further information I needed would be given to me before the class started — and I was right.

The following evening more and more people crammed into the room for the new term. Over fifty people turned up by word of mouth, twice the number that were in the previous class. Some had driven for over two hours to get there and I remember thinking that angels must have been very busy talking into people's ears. Exactly as instructed I introduced the participants to the angels and they all felt their presence. Almost everyone was aware of the angels physically touching them. I was overjoyed.

Since that time I have been on an exciting and illuminating, sometimes challenging, spiritual journey. I have travelled all over the world introducing people to angels and the spiritual beings of the universe. In 2002 I set up the Diana Cooper School to train people to teach about angels, ascension, transformation and Atlantis. This has now expanded and we run courses for angel teachers world wide. The School also facilitates Angel Awareness Day annually and angel events are held on every continent.

Because the frequency on Earth is changing so much the angelic tasks have also changed and there are new Archangels being appointed who are working with us.

I have learnt a great deal from the angels, writing a book a year under their direction. These include more books on angels as well as one on the *Spiritual Laws*. There is *Golden Atlantis* and three novels based on that special era, when everyone was in contact with their angel.

The Unicorns, those magnificent seventh dimensional brings, are part of the angelic hierarchy. They are connecting with people now to help raise our frequency, so I was overjoyed when they asked me to write *The Wonder of Unicorns*.

With the advent of digital cameras angelic beings have been able to impress their light bodies onto film, where they appear as circles known as Orbs. At last angels can be seen by the naked eye. *Enlightenment Through Orbs* and *Ascension Through Orbs* are filled, not only with information but also with stunning, life changing pictures of Orbs!

So when Findhorn Press asked me to update and expand *A Little Light on Angels* into this book, *A New Light on Angels*, I immediately realised it was time. I have endeavoured to keep the purity and simplicity of the original book, while adding more stories and examples. I offer new information about the way angels can help us and I also outline the higher angels, archangels and universal angels who are now working with humanity. This includes how and where we can most easily connect with them, so it is very exciting.

The whole planet and all people and animals on her are starting to ascend with the help of the angels. I hope this book will inspire you, uplift you and help you on your path.

CHAPTER 1

What Are Angels?

"What exactly are angels?" I asked the three angels in front of me as I sat on the bed with a towel round me, after they appeared while I was in the bath.

My angelic instructor told me that angels are high spiritual beings. He said that Source (or God) appoints angels as guides, protectors and helpers for His creation and uses them as His messengers.

Most humans are less highly evolved spirits, who are in a physical body for this experience on Earth.

Everyone and everything is made up of vibrations. The heavier the vibration, the denser the object, which is why chairs, tables and humans can be seen and felt.

Angels have a lighter, faster vibration, so they are usually invisible to us humans.

They are androgynous beings beyond the need for sexuality as their masculine and feminine aspects are perfectly in balance. When a perfect balance of the masculine and feminine energies is achieved in human beings of either sex, they are beyond sexual desire. Only very evolved humans reach this level which is why celibacy is so difficult for most humans. Those who *strive* to be celibate clearly are not ready.

Where are angels in the spiritual scheme of things? Generally they are of a much faster frequency than we are, though just like humans they vary in their spiritual growth according to the level of enlightenment they have reached.

Humans are evolving on one pathway and angels on another, for angels come from the heart of God while humans come from the mind of God. I am frequently asked if a person can be an angel and every time I ask, the answer is 'No.'

My angelic instructor told me that some angels are here to serve and help humankind. Dogs, cats and many animals often serve humans too, yet they are also on their own separate evolutionary path.

It would not normally serve a human soul to return to Earth as a dog, nor would it serve a dolphin's growth to become a human. So angels, dolphins, humans, dogs and other creatures usually evolve on their own pathways and part of their growth takes place as they interact with other species.

There are many different kinds of angels, just as there are many races of humans, each learning and growing in its own way. There are angels who dedicate themselves to healing, others to promoting love, peace, happiness or many qualities.

Angels come to each couple at their marriage ceremony. There are angels of commitment, angels of joy, peace, love, celebration and many others. Their task is to help the couple and encourage them to stay together. Even after a married couple splits up, their angels may still be trying to bring them together. This is one reason why we need a divorce ceremony, so that the angels can be released to do other work.

And yes, we do all have a guardian angel who connects with us at birth or sometimes at conception, and stays near us. Like our spirit guides, they can only feel as close as we allow them to. Often they cannot get through the turbulent vibrations of our emotions to reach us and enfold us.

There are small angels, who look after small tasks, and enormous angels with inconceivably vast energy, who oversee great universal projects.

You will invariably find angels round churches and cathedrals. They are also present whenever people meet for religious or spiritual purposes. Angels gather at power points on the planet. These are often places of great beauty and here their presence can be felt.

There are huge angels in charge of the vast mountain ranges, forests, stars and suns. There are enormous angels out in space.

Throughout the ages, even in primitive times, artists consciously or unconsciously have tuned into them and depicted in their pictures and sculptures all the different kinds of angels.

And angels do sing. They are not called choirs of angels by chance. The mystics and spiritual masters throughout history must have seen and heard them, and passed the information on to those who were ready to hear. Angels create divine celestial music, mostly sounds which are beyond the human auditory range. Nevertheless, the heavenly sounds affect us, uplift, inspire and heal us. These sounds touch the very cells of our being and change us whether we are aware of it or not.

The very presence of angels amongst us opens the gates of our consciousness to greater possibilities. And there are more with us now than at any previous time in history. The reason for this is that our planet has reached a critical point. We have despoiled it and surrounded it with an almost impenetrable force of negativity. The Creator has decreed that this cannot continue. We are not to be allowed to destroy the beautiful Earth. This would cause an imbalance in the universe.

So now humans must raise their consciousness to a level where they honour the Earth, nature, all species of animals and each other — or they must leave.

Angels are flocking here now

to help us all

rise in consciousness.

CHAPTER 2

Angels Are Waiting To Help

Angels have such great love that they respond when we send out cries from the depth of our soul. They also respond to the wishes of our hearts. Their compassion for planet Earth and all the animals and humans on her is resulting in them appearing in great numbers to help us in these times of turbulence, distress and change.

I received the following letter from Patricia O'Flaherty who writes about an incident which occurred during a period of deep and profound unhappiness.

> *I was sitting alone in the night, sobbing and feeling so alone and wretched, when I suddenly 'heard', "You are not alone. We're here", and became aware of a host of kindly angelic forces in the room with me, warm and loving and moving quietly about, all around me. It cheered me and consoled me and since then, I realise we never are as alone as we perceive ourselves to be.*

If our need is great enough, angels will be there to comfort, guide and sometimes even help us physically.

In *The Power of Inner Peace*, I tell the story of a friend of mine who I call Barry in the book. He had been working tremendously long hours to maintain his business. Night after night he drove home in a state of exhaustion, hardly able to keep his eyes open. One night the inevitable happened and, just before he reached a busy major roundabout, he fell asleep at the wheel. When he opened his eyes with a start, he had negotiated the roundabout and was driving down the road.

In the seat beside him sat an angel, holding the steering wheel and guiding the car. As soon as he woke, the angel disappeared, leaving him feeling amazed and awed.

I believe that we are constantly being protected by our guardian angels and other spiritual helpers. How else could we, with our limited mortal senses, race down motorways at immense speed and miss each other? Who protects daredevil little children? Greg chatted to a cleaner at work about guardian angels. She stopped to think, then said, 'That makes sense. I often wondered how my boys survived?'

Usually angels are invisible to us because they vibrate on a level beyond the range of human vision. Sometimes we can raise our consciousness sufficiently to perceive them. On other occasions, because we are in a relaxed or sleepy state, the veil between the worlds becomes thin and we see them.

Most often we simply sense their presence and the impulse of energy from nowhere which helps us. As I was writing this chapter a friend was telling me of her mother, who is a very cautious and down-to-earth person. She was struggling to lift an impossibly heavy wardrobe. Suddenly there was a warm rush of air and she felt the wardrobe being lifted by unseen hands. She 'knew' it was an angel.

There are many references in the Bible to angels coming to people bringing messages during sleep. This still happens but many refer to these visitations simply as dreams — a figment of our imagination. How the spiritual worlds must wonder at us humans!

Catriona told me that she and her husband had booked tickets for a concert in Belfast that they had been longing to hear for ages. Of course, they paid in advance. They decided to make it really special and go to town for the whole weekend and stay with friends. The tickets duly arrived and to their consternation they discovered the concert was on the Wednesday not the Saturday as they had understood. They were bitterly disappointed as all the arrangements had been made and they could not change their day.

Catriona lit a candle and sat down to talk to the angels. She told them what had happened and said she very much wanted to go to the concert. Then she added, 'Angels, it's up to you.' Two days later she received notification that the date of the concert had been moved to Saturday!

A friend of mine was petrified of flying. When she did try to face her fear, she had a terrifying and debilitating panic attack on the plane. For years, this had stopped her from travelling as she would like to do.

We asked for spiritual help for her, knowing that help will always come when we ask, whether we recognise it and accept it or not.

That night she dreamt that she was on a plane which was being held up by a huge golden angel. She woke knowing she had been told that it was completely safe for her to travel. She is now a confident frequent flyer. Since I have been taking Orb pictures, I have been astonished that every single photo I have snapped of a plane has angel Orbs surrounding it, usually bigger than the plane itself. They are always looking after us.

Sometimes angels even come to us and give us healing during our sleep state. A young woman called Sharon wrote and told me of her healing experience.

Her right knee had become quite painful and she did not know why. She had been to her doctor, who had examined it and given her some medication. She went to bed without taking the medication, planning to start it in the morning.

That night she dreamt that she was lying on her stomach and her legs were weightless. They just floated up. They were still attached to her body and were a little way off the ground. This was a lovely sensation. Then golden hands, just hands, were massaging both of her legs. This too felt wonderful.

The next morning her knee felt much better and, over the next couple of days, the pain went completely. She never needed the medication.

It will be a different world

when we all call in angels

to help us with our healing.

CHAPTER 3

Spiritual Experiences

Lesley came to my Life Purpose workshop and shared this story of the spiritual experience which set her on a pathway, seeking and searching for the truth.

Three years earlier she had a very emotional and traumatic year of multiple personal losses. As she reeled under shock after shock, she sat and tried to work out the meaning of life. This is what she wrote to me about what subsequently happened.

> *A week later, while I was sleeping in the early hours of morning, I was awoken by a very bright 'white light'. It was like nothing I had ever seen before on Earth — so bright it 'lit' the whole of my bedroom up. It was not a normal light. I had never encountered something like this before!*
>
> *It did not make me squint like the sun or car headlights. It was a radiating, bright, 'pure white' light (not blinding but 'glowing') and it was giving out this beautiful warm feeling of love, as if to tell me not to be afraid. I kept looking at this 'being of light' and it made me feel so loved and seemed to say, "You know what I'm here for — believe in me."*
>
> *I remember waiting to see if I was going to get a message, and what was going to happen next. The next thing I remember is I saw myself looking down from the ceiling at my body in bed. It was incredible. Then before I knew it, I was back in my body in bed, pulling the duvet cover over my head.*
>
> *It was amazing. I could not forget it, so I started reading books and found out I had seen the 'being of light' and had an out-of-body experience.*

Whenever humans are visited by angels, they report an overwhelming feeling of love and peace. Angels do come to reassure us and give us the impetus to move forward.

I often find that when I share my spiritual experiences with people they respond by sharing theirs. On one occasion I was chatting to a young man who told me that he had been in the depths of despair at the break up of a relationship. It was as if his whole heart and soul had been torn apart and he could see no future. All he could see was blackness and he remained in the darkness of this pit for a long time.

Then one night he was looking bleakly out of the window at a tree. Gradually the tree became lighter and lighter until he could only see a radiant light with a face in it. He had a sense of peace and for the first time felt it was possible to live again. From that moment he began to pick up the threads of his life again. He was sure the face was that of his guardian angel.

A young woman, who had M.E. for many years, attended one of my workshops. She met the angels and had several healing experiences.

Next day she wrote to me with the following story:

Angels have healed me in the past on an emotional level and made miraculous differences, so I thought maybe they could heal me on a physical level and give me grace to release my post viral fatigue! It would certainly be a miracle, as this has been going on for a few years now.

So I lay down to meditate and as I did so, I felt a large angel at my head, holding one hand either side of my head. Obviously the intention was enough to draw the angels close.

I asked to be taken to Source and given grace to release my illness. At Source I was lying down, covered in a white cloth. There were lots of angels around me — at least 20, and still the angel was at my head. I could see bright golden light shining between the angels who were dressed in white.

I heard trumpets blowing and looked up and there were two angels floating above me. I got the names Cherubim and Seraphim and have since found out they are high frequency angels. At the time I was not even sure if they were angel names.

I asked why the trumpets were blowing and I was told, "Because you are special."

I asked for grace to release my illness and a Godforce in the form of a white mist came over and through me from my toes right up to my head to release negativity. This happened four times.

Then I was infused with a golden beam of light from head to toe. I could see an amazing bright golden, sparkling beam of light coming to my head but at first it couldn't get in. So the angels used a liquid to clear a channel down my spine. The light, once in, gradually spread around to all the cells of my body. I particularly felt it in the upper body.

I wanted to stay at Source to really allow the healing to start working. I then felt immense heat in my head and particularly around the back of my neck at the top of my spine. The heat was inside me. The angel was still at my head. Then after a few minutes my head completely cleared and I felt really peaceful. It was like a sudden release.

I had a long thin cross of light placed over my body. Then I came down from Source and into my heart centre and into my body. I was told to rest for seven days.

Afterwards I felt really peaceful. All my worries, anxieties and thoughts were gone.

Ask for healing and

the angels will help.

CHAPTER 4

Angel Signs

Angels are round us all the time but most people cannot see them. For this reason they leave signs for us to assure us of their presence. Birds, butterflies and feathers are some of the commonest signals they give us. Little white feathers are becoming well recognised as messages from the angels.

I have heard many stories of people asking for a sign from the angels or for help from their guardian angels, and being left a white feather in a totally inaccessible place. Bill told me that he really wanted the job for which he had an interview but there were many applicants. He asked the angels to give him a sign that he was right for the job and when he got back into his car, there was a little white feather sitting on the driving seat. He knew instantly that he would be offered the post and he was.

Lila is one of the angel teachers of the Diana Cooper School. She told me the terribly sad story of her oldest daughter whose first baby was stillborn. The entire family had so much wanted this baby and they were all devastated at the loss. Lila tried to support her daughter but she herself was heartbroken.

A few days after the death of the child she went to a book shop to collect a book she had ordered. She was still grieving and asked the angels for a sign to help her. While the book was being fetched, she saw one about angels and picked it up. On the first page were written the words, 'To Lila. We love you. The angels are with you.'

What a sign! It helped her enormously.

Jacqui's husband died after many happy years of marriage and she was naturally devastated. She hardly knew what to do with herself. To try to recover she went to Loch Derg, a place of pilgrimage in Donegal, Ireland. Here she fasted for three days and during this time she kept seeing little white feathers. She was sure they must mean something and in her heart she felt they were a message from her husband. She told the Prior and he lent her a CD to listen to. It transpired to be *A Little*

Light on Angels in which I talk about white feathers. Jacqui told me that when she heard this, she knew she wasn't going mad and she danced for joy. That was when she decided to train to be an angel teacher.

Jacqui also told me another story. She was already a widow when an elderly neighbour died, leaving her husband, Michael, a widower. He and Jacqui often talked about death. One day she called on him and found him reading *A Little Light on Angels*, which he said was very interesting – but he wanted a sign to give him confirmation. His daughter arrived with a newspaper folded so that only two eyes were showing. Jacqui said to me, 'He looked at it and knew it was you, Diana. Then he realised that was the acknowledgement he was seeking.'

One day Michael said to Jacqui, 'I'll go first Jacqui and I'll send you a sign.' A year later Michael died suddenly and after she had been to his house, Jacqui went home and lay on the sofa in front of the TV and cried. She told him she wanted that sign from him that he had promised. She needed cheering up so she put on a Rosemary Connelly video. In the background was playing, 'You and I have a guardian angel on high.' She went into the kitchen and put on the radio. It was playing, 'You and I have a guardian angel on high.'

That afternoon she walked down the beach and saw her sister in a coffee shop. She told her the story but her sister said that there was probably a very good explanation for the coincidence. However, her sister's friend loved angels and she was convinced that it was a message from Michael. As if to confirm this, when Jacqui got home the song was playing on the radio again. The following day there was a free CD in the paper with – guess what – the same song again!!

I think Michael got his message through.

It was the anniversary of Joan's husband's death and she felt very emotional. She took her beloved husband's picture off the piano and said to him, 'Where are you, Sid?' As she said that a little white feather fell from nowhere and she absolutely knew he was alright.

~ *Coincidence and Synchronicity* ~

Coincidences and synchronicities are other less tangible signs that the angels are working with you. We live in an ordered universe where nothing happens by chance.

All those lucky meetings or opportune happenings are orchestrated by our guides and angels. They work very hard to make sure we bump into the right person or read that particular paragraph or hear that story on the radio at the exact moment we need to.

As I was writing this I looked back through some old e-mails and laughed when I came across this one from Inga. She wrote: 'I have never sent a letter to an author before but felt I had to tell you how much I enjoyed your book *A Little Light on the Spiritual Laws* and tell you about a crazy coincidence/synchronicity in my life that is connected in a small way to your book.

Remember at the end of Chapter 3 - The Law of Request, how you mention your daughter driving a car while feeling exhausted? She needed help re-energizing and saw a vehicle with "AUM" in the number plate which made her feel better. Well, I remember reading this and thinking that it was a poor example of the Law of Request and that you could read almost anything into any number plate and how seeing something like that is hardly a message from the universe. (Yes, I was being a wee bit judgmental - something I am working on).

Well anyway, today I was driving along pondering my own question, when would you believe it, a car drove in front of me with the number plate "AUM"!!

'*I was stunned and I had to laugh because of the connection to your book and my judgmental reaction to it. As I was chuckling to myself another car passed in front of me with the word "JOY" on its number plate. Now, I don't know, but I felt that the universe was having a bit of fun with me. In any case it brightened my day and prompted me to email you.*

There are no coincidences.

Everything is orchestrated

by the angels.

CHAPTER 5

Guardian Angels

Our guardian angel is with us throughout all our lives. It comes to us at birth or sometimes at conception, so no-one walks their path on planet Earth alone. If only we knew how much help there is around us in the spirit world, we would not feel so vulnerable and isolated. Often it is only at times of crisis that we become aware of the presence of this help.

Mary Miller wrote to me of her son's experience with his guardian angel.

> *My angel story goes back to 1980 when my son started to drive. One night when he had not arrived home by midnight I was over overanxious for his safety. Then an inner voice from wherever prompted me to put his guardian angel on duty. Immediately my anxiety was replaced by a sound sleep.*
>
> *At breakfast the following morning my son told me of a strange experience on his way home. Within a mile from home he nodded off to sleep. Then he heard a strange voice call his name — in his words — 'not yours, Mam or Dad's or any voice I know. But I will certainly recognise it, should I ever hear it again.'*
>
> *To this day we are both convinced it was his guardian angel. Needless to say, I am on very good terms with angels ever since. May the Divine Assistance remain always with us.*

I love the story that Mary shared. It shows how we are all linked so deeply. If every mother who worried about her child would ask the child's guardian angel to protect it — and then relax and trust the protection, the world would be a lighter and safer place.

Most parents think they are being good parents when they worry about their children. They are not. Worry is a heavy, dense, negative vibration. When we direct it with force towards our beloved child, who is psychically linked to us, we open our child to disease, danger and negative influences. Black, brooding fear and worry energy can make a sensitive child ill.

When we send love, healing and positive thoughts to our child, we surround our offspring with a protective, joyous force. If we also ask our child's guardian angel to protect him or her, our love energy opens the way for it to link more closely to the child.

Of course, we can do this for anyone, whether a friend or a stranger. Love is the energy that opens the hearts of others and we direct the love energy with our thoughts. When we send pure love to people, the angelic forces can link into them to activate miracles. It is also powerful if we direct the angels to help.

Listen to your intuition and send love to people in need, in danger, pain or grief. If you pass a hospital, ask the healing angels to help those in need. Your loving intercession allows the angels to get closer and heal more effectively.

Angels heal animals too. If you know of an animal in distress, ask an angel to help it. It will speed the animal's recovery.

When you think of a war zone, do not focus on the bad things happening there. This energises the darkness. Instead picture peace coming into the area. Ask the angels to help the people there. Your prayers become pathways of light for the angels to enter and assist.

If we hear, read about or see bad news in the media, we can pause for a moment and send light to the person or area. This assists more than we have any concept of. The love and light we send can avert disasters, or help and heal others.

When someone is taking an exam, ask the angels to be with them, then picture their success. If a friend is moving house, travelling, starting a new business or undertaking any challenge, visualise it going well with the angels surrounding them. It takes more energy to envision disaster or bad outcomes than it does happiness, abundance or wonderful things happening.

Every single one of us plays an important role on the planet. You may think your little bit makes no difference but when added to energy others are sending, it creates a vast wave of light which can help to make massive changes for the betterment of people and places.

Evil, or the terrible feeling of being separate from Source, as I prefer to see it, is afraid of light and love. Sending waves of love to the minds of 'evil' people and leaders, who place personal power above the happi-

ness of their people, will wash out the need for control and abuse and allow freedom to return.

When we send loving

thoughts to others,

we create bridges of light

for angels to walk along.

CHAPTER 6

Angels Are In Service

After the angels appeared to me, I was very excited about the Healing and Psychic Development class they had impressed on me to run. I hoped that I could keep my vibration steady enough for the angels to come close.

My angel instructor told me that they work on a golden ray and indeed I saw the healing angels as whitish gold colour - the same shade as the one who came to me in my moment of soul despair. He said, "Gold is the colour of wisdom and truly unconditional love. When you are healing with these angels, it is a golden energy. Angelic energy has a sunshine warmth and no angel will ever make you feel cold when it is near you."

He added that angels are in service and that when you work with angelic energy you identify yourself with being in service.

So at the class we sat quietly and imagined ourselves filling the room with gold light until we were in a solid golden space.

Before the class started I had been told to ask everyone to stroke their own aura with their hands. After this we were to invite angels to stroke our auras. This would give us the opportunity to feel the loving energy of the angelic beings waiting to help us all.

So I asked everyone to do both of these things. We can gradually bring our hands closer to our bodies until we feel the slight resistance or tingling feeling of the edge of our aura. It is a practical way to smooth over any holes or uneven places in our energy fields so that we are more protected. Most people experienced it as calmly soothing.

Our aura is our protective electromagnetic shield, which is created by our thoughts. Wishy-washy thoughts mean that we have a weak aura which does not protect us from the actions or thoughts of others. Strong, positive and loving thoughts ensure a solid protective aura. Negative thoughts make holes in our auras, while if we are in shock, our aura often disappears and we are then vulnerable to outside forces.

Most of us have seen pictures of saints, gurus and holy people with beautiful golden halos around their heads or with light round their bodies. These are the emanations of their pure and spiritual thoughts as seen by those with psychic eyes.

In that first class many of us could see a ring of angels round the room, who had drawn near in response to our expectation. Each participant invited one of the angels to stroke their aura. This proved to be a very different experience from smoothing their own aura. It felt very powerful and several people burst into tears.

One of the class members shared what had happened to her. She told us that she had had a blinding headache all day and desperately wanted an angel to come to her. She thought an angel would help her headache but none would come to her. Instead a cherub played around her. It was smiling and absolutely delightful but it kept swishing about above her head.

She kept saying to it, "Stroke my aura," but it just smiled and played above her head. The more frustrated she became, the more the cherub smiled and wafted over her. However, when the cherub waved and left at the end of the exercise, her headache had gone completely!

There were several experienced healers in this class, so I asked them to let go of all preconceptions and other methods of healing, empty their minds and put their hands on the aura of the person they were working with, allowing the angels to work through them. Most of them were astonished. They felt the power of the angels flowing through them.

A similar thing happens when we open ourselves up as a channel for spiritual healing. The clearer a channel we are the more divine healing energy flows through us. However the healing with the angels felt quite different. It actually felt golden.

Here is what one of the participants wrote to me afterwards.

> *When you introduced us to angels at the healing class, I could really feel a very light but powerful energy. I particularly enjoyed going with the angels and the lady I was healing up to Source for healing energy. Since then I have asked the angels to come to me every day. Although I can't see them, I can always feel their warm, loving presence and they have seen me through some rough times! I asked them to be there when I came for a session with you and they came and, I feel, performed the most miraculous healing!*

Angels heal in a light way.

CHAPTER 7

The Healing Power Of Forgiveness

I first met Lynfa Davies at one of my Healing with Angels workshops. I noticed her immediately as she radiated a glow of warmth and happiness.

During the course of the workshop she shared this story. She had been raped when she was thirteen. Her marriage had broken up and so had the following relationship which had been very abusive. The pain around these memories was pretty intense, so much so that counselling and similar therapies seemed very threatening.

She realised that she had a choice. She could continue to exist with the pain and hurt or she could find a way of letting it go and forgiving, so that she could live again.

She chose rebirthing because it is much less intellectual and mind-based than many therapies and decided that it is indeed possible to heal anything — however painful. With this intention she worked with her rebirther. This is what she wrote about her subsequent experience.

Following this decision, I started to get what I thought was indigestion — really severe pains around my heart. During the next session, I was breathing as usual and I suddenly heard and felt wings just above my head. Everything became very calm and in my mind's eye I saw large, white wings around me. I felt completely engulfed by them, completely safe and then I saw a man's face looking down at me. He looked rather like the angels from Wim Wender's film "Wings of Desire" — fierce, strong and very gentle.

He told me that my heart was broken, and that it had been for a long time, and that he had come to put it together again. I felt a very warm feeling in and around my heart — an enormous energy and also a feeling of peace and knowing that things were OK and I was safe. At the end of the session the pain had gone, and I can now talk about being raped very much more easily, with no pain.

I am a pretty down-to-earth sort of person — but since this session I have been using angel cards and feel very protected and cared for, which is definitely a new thing for me.

**When we put out our intentions and are open
to all possibilities miracles happen.**

Annie Rossiter shared this story of what happened to her after a workshop.

I had been to one of your workshops, Diana. My father had abused me as a child and I was looking at why I had chosen the parents I had. It was while I was doing this that I realised how much anger I was holding onto towards him.

You helped me to let that go. That in itself was quite an amazing experience. I got home and felt shaken but not unpleasantly so. I just needed to meditate and be still and quiet. Having let go of the anger, I felt empty. Although you had got me to breathe in love, I wanted more. I needed love to fill my emptiness where the anger had been.

I lay on the bed and became very quiet. I began to hear a noise, a very soft noise, like the rustling of feathers. Then in my mind I saw white angels with beautiful white wings and I had a great sense of love filling me.

This had a profound effect on me. The anger is not there any more. Before I was blaming my father for my life. Now all the blame has gone.

Angels can fill our hearts with love.

CHAPTER 8

Angels And Children

Before their memory banks close down in the heavy vibration of planet Earth, children often communicate with the spirit world and they can frequently recall their past lives. One mother told me her three-year-old said to her one day, "You know Mummy, it's funny having these legs. They were brown before."

Many children, especially those who have no siblings or who are lonely, play with invisible friends. These friends, children from the spirit world, are unseen by adult eyes but perfectly real and visible to those little ones who can still see the spiritual realms. Youngsters are also open to seeing fairies and angels.

In an infant, the right brain, our intuitive, psychic and imaginative side, is naturally open to such experiences. This is the side of our brain which governs healing, mediumship, creative and artistic work. However, in our culture, we lean heavily towards logical thinking and numerate school work, with emphasis on competition and success. When, at the age of five, our offspring enter such an education system, inevitably their natural intuition, creativity and imagination shut down. Between the ages of five and ten, most children cease to commune with spirit children, fairies and angels.

> *It will transform planet Earth when we honour the equal development of the right and left brain.*
> *Then we will have superhumans, who can access much more of their potential and live at a greater level of awareness.*

Jeanne Slade told me her story in a lovely, lilting Welsh accent. Like so many Celts, she is a natural psychic and has been for as long as she can remember. The eldest of four children she was born and brought up in a cottage in the heart of Wales. The number of the cottage was 33. Every house number has a vibration. She told me that the number 11 is especially good for the development of intuition, clairvoyance and psychic ability. A house number 22 has the vibration of unlimited potential and to live in a house numbered 33 means that all things are possible! It is also the frequency that resonates with Christ Consciousness, while 44 aligns with the golden era of Atlantis.

As a dreamy, psychic child she saw and communed with angels. Her mother lacked understanding and often sent her to her room, where she spent much time alone. When she spoke of the angels to her grandmother, she told her not to tell lies! It was very confusing for the child to be told that her reality was a falsehood. Nevertheless she continued to gain comfort from the presence of her guardian angel.

Then when she was seven years old, the quiet, sensitive child was abused by her teacher at school. From that moment she never saw her guardian angel again. In the trauma of losing her innocence and her spiritual support, she suppressed the memories of what had happened and of the angels.

As an adult, during therapy, full memory of the abuse returned. She finally exorcised the pain in the only possible way, by genuine forgiveness of the perpetrator. At the moment of forgiveness she exclaimed, "Oh, I can see my angel again."

She came to realise that, in the way of children, she thought the abuse was her fault and she must be bad for such a thing to happen so she did not tell anyone. She felt that she did not deserve a guardian angel and because of this belief she could not see it any more.

Jeanne's daughter, who is a practising clairvoyant, was able to communicate with the grandmother, who was in spirit. The grandmother told her that she had sent a guide to help Jeanne with the regression because she felt very guilty about her childhood.

It transpired that Jeanne's grandmother was also psychic. When she was telling Jeanne as a child not to tell lies about the angels, she could in fact see them herself.

Presumably when she was on Earth, the old lady thought she would be helping the child to be more 'normal and acceptable' if she denied the presence of the angels. From the wider perspectives of the spirit world, she realised the damage she had done and had orchestrated the healing in order to make amends.

Now, although Jeanne has not 'seen' the angels since, she has felt and experienced the enormous love of their presence.

Such stories from childhood often remind me of the tale of The Emperor's Clothes. In this story a pair of villains told the courtiers that they were spinning magic cloth. If the buyers were honest and worthy, they would be able to see the splendid material, but if the buyers should be stupid and dishonest, then the material would be invisible. No-one wished to admit that they could not see the expensive clothes for which they were being measured. The emperor himself pretended he could see his new clothes because he thought everyone would realise he was stupid and dishonest if he admitted he could not see them. So he went out into the town without clothes, while everyone pretended to admire them in case they should be considered the stupid and dishonest ones. Only a child called out, "The Emperor isn't wearing any clothes."

Where many an adult will deny

that they can see an angel

for fear of being ridiculed,

a child in its innocence

will speak the truth.

CHAPTER 9

Peace Angels

I had never even heard of peace angels but when I saw them I knew immediately who they were. They were larger than the healing angels and a different colour. These beautiful luminous beings were creamy white and fluffy with large, soft wings. I can't describe them in any other way. They were warm and felt feathery and incredibly calm.

A few days after I first became aware of these angels, I was running a course on inner peace. Presumably that is why they appeared to me. One of the participants, a most pleasant and charming man, worked in the city. I felt sure that he had come to an inner peace workshop to de-stress himself and would have no concept of the spiritual realms.

During one exercise I became aware of one of the peace angels standing behind him, enfolding his solar plexus with her wings. For an instant I considered whether or not to say anything. I certainly did not want to frighten him. On the other hand, I did not want to miss an opportunity which might be important for him. So I said to him that a peace angel had her wings round him and if he cared to lean back into her she would hold him. Without hesitation he did so and afterwards told me that it was a wonderful comforting experience. He felt inspired and delighted by it.

I do hope he took the peace back into the city.

A few months later I was again about to teach a weekend course on inner peace. I was in my local swimming pool thinking about the course and my mind must have become relaxed and receptive for suddenly a voice said:

"We want you to impart an important message to those whom we've brought together this weekend.

Peace must be spread and it can only start within individuals who are ready to forgo their power struggle with others. Peace is surrender to spirit, not proving you are better than another."

"Impress on each one to make a corner of their home into a peace corner. This doesn't mean candles or crystals or rituals. It means a space in which you think only peaceful thoughts. It may be as small as one chair in the house but having chosen the spot never approach it unless your thoughts are centred and peaceful. That little corner is like an acorn of peace. It will sprout and grow through slender sapling into a vast protective oak which will fill and protect your home.

"Start by planting one peace acorn in your home. Then little by little plant others in other places. With other like minded souls choose a spot. It may be outside a particular shop in your High Street or a corner of your town. Whenever you are near, enter this small space with peaceful thoughts. Even if it is only for a moment, you are planting and nurturing a peace place.

"Many, but not all, trees are anchors for peace on planet Earth. If you are centred and calm and you pass such a tree, pause, breathe peace out to the tree and breathe peace back in from it. This will help to strengthen the peace points on the planet and will help you to become an anchor point for peace — someone who can spread peace."

It is spiritual law that whatever we focus on increases. The peace angel impressed on me,

Focus on peace and fear will dissolve.

Focus on love and hate will disappear.

Focus on joy and grief will evaporate.

Cultivate flowers

and weeds cannot take hold.

CHAPTER 10

Spiritual Oil

One message from the angelic peace bearers was,

"You cannot be at peace while you give anyone or anything power over you. If anyone has any influence over your thoughts and feelings — to the extent that they affect you, you are not at peace."

When we are in a solid unbroken aura, we are totally protected and, of course, no one can influence us. If our aura is broken at any point because of our negative thoughts, we are vulnerable and then it is difficult to feel peaceful. An aura made strong by our own powerful and positive thoughts is impregnable. Then we feel safe.

Angels can and do come in and stroke our auras if we ask them to. This immediately strengthens the aura and helps to protect us.

Again and again the angels tell me that they are waiting to help but we must ask them to. We can even ask them to help others and they will willingly do so. They respond to our energy. If you are driving down the road and you hear an ambulance siren, ask for extra angelic help for the person in need. You do not know what force for good you set in motion.

The peace angels reminded me about a recent client whom I shall call George and added the reminder that they were always ready and willing to work in this way with people if only we invite them to.

George was a very good man, spiritual and well-intentioned, but in turmoil. He felt powerless and was full of feelings of anger and rage. Negative emotions make holes in our aura and because his protective aura was full of holes he had no energy and had become physically ill. He was seeking the cause of this problem.

He told me that in a past life under torture, he had betrayed his people. When I started working with him, I closed my eyes and immediately saw a picture of him with hundreds of cords, like hosepipes, attached to him.

When I followed one of these cords, I saw at the other end a crowd of people surrounded in darkness. The dark energy was the fear and anger of those people he had betrayed. Each one of them still had a cord hooked into him. Even now their fear and rage was flowing through it like sludge through a pipe.

Of course, if his aura had been solid and unbroken, these cords could not have penetrated his space but his guilt and anger let them in. Whether these people were incarnate or not, these lines were still active. Also active were the lines of anger which attached him to his enemies.

Because all these unhealthy cords were piercing his aura, he could never make it strong and peaceful, so he was vulnerable to negative influences.

The angel said to me, "As you know, we angels were waiting, longing to help. All week before he came for his session with you, he felt the importance of it but he didn't know why. It was because you were calling on us — angels of light — to help.

When you first asked for grace, you set powerful wheels in motion — and the dispensing of a spiritual oil. We angels were so joyful to be asked — as you saw. While you held the energy, we were able to release all those cords and take those souls into the light."

When it is time for someone to die, angels do help them onto the next stage of their journey. Our prayers greatly help. Certain souls get stuck, either because they are too attached to the material world or because they are consumed by negative emotions such as lust, greed or anger. Angels also help these souls to make the transition but often they need our energy to intercede. General and specific prayers to help such souls are much appreciated by the universe.

In freeing the souls who had been attached to George the angels enabled him to become stronger, healthier and happier.

Many of us constantly complain about what we do not have or what we do not want. Spiritual law says, "Where thought goes, energy flows". So when we complain and grumble we get more of what we don't want. When we focus on what we do want, it increases.

When we keep saying thank you for what we do have, those good things increase immeasurably. If children say thank you dully and automatically for something or grab for more, their parents feel disinclined to give. But if children, glowing with delight, say thank you from the heart, their parents want to give more and more.

The universal energy is the same. Saying thank you from the heart for the good things in our lives, for the qualities we have, for the gifts and talents bestowed on us allows angels to bring more and more abundance to us. It used to be called counting your blessings.

Saying thank you

cleanses and clarifies your aura.

It is a spiritual oil

which draws abundance

into your life.

CHAPTER 11

Angels Of Ceremony And Ritual

Wherever a contract or vow is made, or a bond is signed, there is at least one angel present.

If anything is celebrated with 'pomp and ceremony' there are literally hosts of angels participating. They help to build up the power of the event and to keep the legalities binding.

At the exchange of vows, the contract is recorded in the akashic records, which is the record of all our thoughts and deeds, good and bad. Then an angel comes in to oversee whatever we have undertaken. In the case of a marriage, for example, an angel will stay with the couple and become the whispered voice of conscience and wise guidance to try to keep them together. The state of being in love is a light state, so when we are in love we are open to the influence of the celestial helpers, whether or not we can see or sense them. This fills lovers with a wonderful sense of joy and elation. With angelic help we see the best in others.

If the marriage was one of convenience or if there was no real commitment by either party, it is not considered spiritually to be a marriage and no angel will be allocated. When our relationships get heavy, we close down and are no longer open to receive the help of our angels, who are still patiently waiting for us to open up to them.

At wedding celebrations there are many angels singing, rejoicing and filling the nuptials with love and heavenly laughter. With the advent of digital cameras angels are impressing themselves as Orbs on film. I have been delighted to see that every anniversary party, wedding or celebration photograph is full of angels attending. In addition they are invariably bringing the spirits of loved ones to enjoy the event. If only we humans could open up more to their presence how much lighter and more fun life would be.

At a christening, or its equivalent in other religions, the angels are always present. Again they rejoice at the party afterwards. They bring joy to the occasion and a boost of energy to help the child on its path.

Any landmark on our Earth journey is celebrated by the angels. They come to births, baptisms, birthday parties, anniversaries, graduations, housewarming parties, new job or promotion parties. They are at Christmas parties or Easter ones. They love parties, by which I do not mean drunken orgies, but genuine celebrations where people gather together to enjoy themselves and say thank you.

If we had separation or divorce celebrations, the angels would attend to add their blessings and energy to our new pathway in life. It would make our lives flow more smoothly.

When we honour and rejoice in our birthday the celestial beings give us a boost throughout the year. After all we were offered a special opportunity to come to Earth and it is the anniversary of our arrival. Souls queue up to inhabit a body on planet Earth because the opportunities for spiritual growth are so great here. Every single day we are offered incredible choices to expand our consciousness. There is no other plane in the universe where souls can grow so quickly. If we realised this and honoured it, we would greet every moment with zest and delight. We would open our eyes each morning with expectation and wonder. How can I grow today? What can I learn? What challenges can I overcome? What fears can I conquer? Thank you for this opportunity.

One year on my birthday I stepped outside and took some pictures of the empty night sky. One of the photographs contained a beautiful green, yellow and blue angel Orb which had opened up like an arc to pour energy towards me. By it was an angel of love. Kathy Crosswell and I wrote *Enlightenment Through Orbs* together and I could see that the Orb was Archangels Raphael and Michael with Wywyvsil, Kathy's guide. We were told that Wywyvsil was bringing love from her to me for my birthday. In fact she did not know it was my birthday but in the spiritual realms everything is known.

Just think how busy the angels are at Christmas taking love to people! Loving thoughts and good wishes are never wasted for the angels will carry them and pour them into the energy fields of the people to whom they are sent. If you take a few minutes over the festive season to send loving thoughts to a lonely person, it could make all the difference to their Christmas.

The angels also bring the spirits of loved ones to visit you, especially at significant times. Whenever I see a photograph of a family gathering, unseen angels are always carrying loved ones to join in the celebration.

In simpler times all rites of passage were celebrated, including the arrival of spring, the coming of the rains and phases of the moon.

The planting of seeds and the harvesting of crops both merited a celebration. The rising sun was greeted with a salutation, so was sunset.

In my last house we always used to hold a full moon meditation in our home which was open to anyone and the angels were always there lifting and directing the energy. They love the sacred energy of ritual.

Angels are present and rejoicing at funerals. To those with eyes to see, the discarding of our physical body and transition into the Light is a time for joy. I was told a story by a psychic called Jack who witnessed his best friend die in an accident. Everyone was crying, screaming and in shock when they realised he had passed but Jack watched his friend joyfully moving towards the angels who had come to meet him.

Most people who die need our prayers and the angels collect these and direct them to help the person who is passing. They often sing to aid the spirit of the departed on their journey.

Angels of ceremony and ritual

are present

at all rites of passage.

CHAPTER 12

Angels Light Up The Dark

Gerard appeared to have everything to live for, a warm and loving girlfriend, a child he adored and some good friends but he had some dark memories. One day he tried to commit suicide. His family were considerably shaken and persuaded him to come for help.

He did come for one session which helped him to feel at peace for six weeks. Then something happened which brought up old childhood memories again. He fell back into depression and panic and came for a second appointment.

This time I could strongly feel the presence of the angels who were in the room, so I talked to him about them. After that I regressed him back into his childhood and this time we invited the angels in to help with the healing.

Suddenly a ring of angels surrounded and poured pure white light into him. It was quite amazing to watch. They dissolved the hurt and pain of the little abused child which he still carried inside him. He started to sob as he experienced their love and compassion. When he stopped he said he felt absolutely wonderful.

Many people are very judgemental about suicide but of course the angels do not judge in any way. I was talking to a man after an event. He told me that his daughter had committed suicide a couple of years ago. I responded that she had heard the call to go home because it was her time. He nodded sagely and said that he had heard exactly the same from a medium he knew. He was sure that his daughter was safe and well and helping from the spirit world.

A friend of mine is a medium who was friendly with a family whose son took his own life. For some time the boy had difficulty finding his way on the other side but now he is helping youngsters who are depressed or doing drugs and teaching them in their sleep that there is a positive side to life. He is doing excellent work and deeply satisfied at a soul level.

The angels remind me to repeat that someone can only commit suicide if their soul, sometimes known as their higher self, and God give permission. If permission is not granted, their guardian angel will step in and prevent them from dying.

On one occasion I took a young man back into his childhood. Spontaneously he slipped into a past life as a woman where he had been violated. Even though he had incarnated this time as a man, he still held the memory and feelings of that abuse within his consciousness.

We worked on the dark feelings of rage and shame which had been suppressed in that lifetime and which still needed to be released. A circle of angels appeared and hovered round him. I suggested that he ask them for healing. They held him very gently and he felt them bearing him up and up to the spiritual light before they healed the hurt.

I know this young man was in crisis over money and had been seeking and searching for healing for years. When he paid at the end of the session, he said, "It has been worth every penny to be taken to heaven."

The gentleness of the angels is something often commented upon. A businessman had a terrible fear of torture. He often visited countries with a reputation for torture and always felt in dreadful danger.

I regressed him to a past life where he was imprisoned in heavy chains and died under torture. As he experienced this, an angel appeared to him and unchained his body. The beautiful compassionate being gave his tortured body healing and took it away *calmly and tenderly*. (Those are his words.) He was very affected by the gentleness of it.

Healing angels

are compassionate

and gentle.

CHAPTER 13

Angels Heal Our Hearts

Angels are willing and ready to help us. They have drawn close to our planet in large numbers and are waiting to be called on. The only thing that stops them is that we are not open to them.

They are happy to assist us with our relationships. Ann was very undecided about her life. She didn't know what to do about her relationship. Her boyfriend was suffering from depression and their relationship was rocky.

To my delight angels came into the room and indicated that they were willing to work with her.

I watched two angels put their hands into her heart, filling and smoothing several cracks with healing light. She relaxed as they worked on her. Then they moved to her solar plexus. I saw them pull out grey fluff. Ann told me that they were pulling out dust, like the congealed dust in a dustbin bag. When the angels had pulled out all the grey fluff and passed it to the light, they filled her solar plexus with a lovely golden light and sealed it in.

Then I was shown that she was to go to a hilltop where she could look down on her life. From there she saw that her energy looked brown like rust and her boyfriend was attached to her with sickly green cords. These cords were going into her throat, choking her.

We asked the angels to go in and dissolve the cords with light, which they did, sending light right into the roots of the cords, so that everything was transmuted. She could feel the strange sensation.

When the cords had all gone, she said she felt odd, as if there was no energy in her body where the cords had been. We all take energy from somewhere. She had been in the habit of plugging into her boyfriend and other people when she needed a boost of energy. Now I suggested that, instead of looking for a fill up of lower energy as she had done in the past, she link into the waiting angels.

As the pure, clear energy entered her, it highlighted for her that she had never had a relationship in which she stood on her own two feet.

She had always been co-dependent and leaning. She said in a small voice, "If I'm not vulnerable, I won't be given love."

When I asked her to sense the quality of love she would receive if she were no longer vulnerable and needy, she experienced that she would receive much more wholesome love and respect.

She visualised what her life would be if she maintained and built upon the feeling of wholeness she had, and she felt for the first time a sense of purpose. She felt huge, strong and confident.

The angels stroked her aura to keep these feelings within her auric space, so that she had the opportunity of consolidating the new qualities. When she opened her eyes, she felt that she could move forward in a much stronger way.

A month later she came back to see me again and said that she had had a warm golden feeling of confidence in her solar plexus ever since the angels had worked on her.

She told me that she had always been very jealous of her partner's friends, even his male friends and would throw a wobbly if he went out with them. After the angels sealed strength and confidence into her solar plexus, her feelings changed dramatically.

A few days after the healing from the angels, her partner's ex girlfriend phoned and said she missed him and wanted to meet up with him. Feeling totally relaxed and unconcerned, Ann had passed him the phone and said, "Why don't you take it into the kitchen where you can have a private chat?"

She had felt untroubled while he was talking to his ex girlfriend. And her new confidence was rewarded. When he came back into the room he said, "I told her I was in a committed relationship and I didn't want to meet her."

Angels help us

in the highest way

for our growth.

CHAPTER 14

Angels Are Everywhere

At the end of one class, I asked the participants to watch out for angels the following week. I was surprised by the response. It appeared that once we are aware and looking, angels appear at all sorts of moments. This does not necessarily mean ethereal beings flying in the sky!

One person felt really depressed. She walked down a street she had walked down a million times and glanced casually up. Above her, looking down at her, was a stone angel with sunlight shining all over it. She had never seen it before. Suddenly she felt warm and safe.

One of my favourite angel stories was very simple. Eileen had been nursing her dying father for some time and he had finally died. She felt very sad and empty as she took flowers to the cemetery. The place was deserted and she stood by the grave for a while reflecting on old memories.

She turned to walk away, wondering where all the helping angels were when a woman appeared from nowhere and moved towards her. The stranger said, "You don't know me, but I know you."

Eileen said, "Oh, who are you?"

"Angela!" the stranger replied and walked away leaving Eileen feeling amazed and much comforted. She knew that the angels were reminding her they were there.

At the end of a special healing workshop, everyone felt touched by the energy that had been flowing through the room. As we linked hands at the end of the session, I became aware that behind each person was standing their guardian angel, their hands on the persons' shoulders, ready to enfold, support and protect them. I asked everyone to be aware of this.

When each person had time to absorb the wonderful feeling, I suggested they visualise a golden bubble around themselves. Afterwards one participant said, "I physically felt my angel's hands on my shoulders and when you asked us to put the golden bubble round us, it stepped back to allow space for the bubble to go round me."

Theresa told me that she was with friends on the way to hear me give a talk in Dublin and they were worried that they wouldn't get there in time as they were stuck in a relentless traffic jam. They asked the angels for help. Within moments a young man on a motorbike drew up beside their car and asked if they needed assistance. They told him the name of the hotel they were looking for. He said, 'Follow me.' So they tailed him through a tangle of backstreets. He was wearing a jacket bearing the name Golden Security. When they arrived in good time at the hotel, they jumped out to thank him.

He told them his name was Gabriel, then roared off!

Angels are always there to help us.

CHAPTER 15

Angels Help Us To Let Go

Debbie arrived to see me in a state of shock. Her mother, with whom she was very close, had been rushed to hospital and was in intensive care where she lay in a coma. Naturally Debbie wanted to wait by her bedside but friends persuaded her to come for her appointment. One of them drove her to my house and waited for her.

No sooner had the session started than angels entered the room. They indicated that she was holding on to her mother and that it was important she detach, or uncord, from her. This would free her mother to decide whether to come back or to pass over. Of course, this felt devastating for Debbie, but she had a high level of spiritual understanding and recognised that it was right.

I relaxed Debbie and asked her to visualise the cords which attached her to her mother. She saw grey chains surrounding them both and we asked the angels to dissolve them. They gently pulled all the chains away, freeing mother and daughter from each other.

When all the chains had been released, Debbie saw that her mother was stronger and she herself felt happy and bigger, as if she had grown.

Later that day, she phoned me to say that, *at the exact moment of uncording, her mother had come off the ventilator and sat up.* She felt that her letting go had been a vital part of this.

A week later her mother died. That week gave them an opportunity to say goodbye properly and I believe that the angels interceded to allow this.

A few days after this a young woman came to me because she could not get away from her family. Her father was an angry bully, who blackmailed her into staying at home by saying that she could never come back if she left. None of the family had been able to escape and they lived in a household of anger, silences and fear.

As she talked about her father, it became very clear that he was holding onto everyone because he was terrified of being left alone. She realised that it was not his wise adult self who was blackmailing and threatening her. When he bullied the family, he was a terrified little five-year-old boy.

For the first time she became aware that her father was desperate about what would happen to him if she left. With that awareness came a tenderness and sense of compassion. Now she understood just how much reassurance and love he really needed.

As I watched, her face softened as her heart opened towards him. She saw that if her father felt she really loved him, he would be quite happy to let her go, knowing that she would always return.

Then an angel took her to look down at the family scene from above. She saw a mass of angry, demanding faces, filled with fear and insecurity. They were all stuck in a black treacly mess and none of them could get out of it. The angel poured golden light into the treacle around her and gradually freed her to swim out of it. We asked the angel to release the rest of the family from the treacle and it did so by pulling out the dark sticky energy and pouring in more gold.

Within a short while her brother left home and she started to feel freer to do what she wanted to do.

Angels are free spirits and

will help us to be free too.

CHAPTER 16

Healing With Angels

When I told her that I was writing a book about angels, one of my clients, a beautiful young lady who had been through a great deal of loss and hardship, sent me the following letter about her experiences during our healing sessions.

~ Angels heal deep wounds ~

I came to you feeling trapped by fear, and feeling very frustrated. I had spent a lot of time in hospital when I was young and had loads of fears of what might happen to me next.

We were doing some inner child work to empower my stuck child. After I had put my empowered three-year-old into my solar plexus, two angels came in to help. They pulled out a really long, black, thick cord from my throat that went right down into my solar plexus. I was amazed because I could actually feel it happening.

Then we moved on to another incident when I was frightened as a six-year-old. The angels came and helped again. They released black smoke from my solar plexus. Then they lifted my six year old, black with smoke, up to Source. It felt so great that I didn't want to come back!

The session was very powerful and I was very happy that I had so much help around. I felt pleased that there is a way of healing deep wounds and changing frustrating patterns in my life.

~ Releasing feelings of abandonment ~

A few weeks later I came to see you again. I had had a terrible week with old emotions surfacing and completely taking hold of me. The main issue was feelings of abandonment — feeling

*unwanted and unloved. I kept waking up in the early hours
of the morning feeling like my heart was tearing apart. The
feelings were so intense and uncomfortable I felt like destroy-
ing myself to ease the pain. I knew these feelings were from the
past and I had done months of inner work on loving myself
but I was at my wit's end.*

*During the session you saw a number of angels with a jug
of golden liquid. They smoothed this over my aura and again
I was amazed as I could actually feel their energy.*

*We then did some inner child work during which the angels
intervened! They wanted to hold my nine-year-old up to the
light. Then they wanted to take me up to Source. You asked
me if I wanted to go up to Source as it would mean purification. I was frightened of going but said I would go as I was at
the end of my tether!*

*So I had to breathe in light and breathe out all sorts of
things including anger, guilt and jealousy. Then I had an
angel on either side and was taken up to Source. On the way
up I felt sick. Then I felt really in the depths of depression
and despair. Then when I got to Source I was to kneel before
the Lords of Karma, who look after the akashic records. They
were to let me resolve this with grace.*

*I had an angel on either side and I could see bright white
light. They put a white cross on my forehead and a hand on
my heart. My attention was drawn to the white cross because
I could feel the warmth and the shape of it in front of my
head — and at that moment all those feelings of sickness and
depression and the tension in my shoulders and neck just
completely washed away!*

*I saw myself kneeling with the white cross on my forehead.
Then I was to come back down. I really wanted to stay and
savour the feeling. It was really lovely, special and holy but
only lasted for a few seconds.*

*I was absolutely amazed at the feelings that I had had! At
the time you said you had never taken anyone to Source like
that before and that I had a lot of help available to me.*

*Since that session I have never had any of those awful
abandonment feelings again and I completely trust the ability
of the angels to heal.*

~ Releasing depression ~

The third spectacular angel healing I had was when I fell into a black hole of depression. It had been going on for two weeks and I tried everything to pull myself out but I kept falling back down that hole.

It was completely engulfing me and affecting my work as everything was out of proportion. At this point I knew the only way out was to call on the angels for help! I came to see you and true to form the angels came along to help!

My small child was in the bottom of a black pit of snakes. The angels removed those snakes, filled the hole in my solar plexus up with golden light and lifted my child up into the light.

It seemed so simple, yet it was incredibly powerful as the depression went completely, straight away!

Since then I have been hooked on angels! I often ask for healing from them and for their help. I have never seen one clearly but have had the impression of a whole group of rainbow-coloured angels lifting me up to the light and I can always feel their warm energy. They have even healed my horse when he was choking.

So thank you very much for introducing me to angels!

She no longer needs to come to me as an intermediary. She can now invite in the angels herself to do the healing.

Call on angels for healing

and they will come to you.

CHAPTER 17

Angels Of Colour

Medical doctors use ultrasound to shake out the negative energy locked into painful joints. They use ultraviolet rays to penetrate and release certain conditions in the body. We know that the use of sound and colour in this way can effectively heal. However, that is a very violent use of sound and colour, rather like taking a mallet to crack a nut.

Every colour has its own vibration and energy which affects us unconsciously even if we are unaware at a conscious level. Bright red will energise us, while green will balance and blue will soothe. Yellow helps us with concentration and indigo will calm the mind. The colours we paint our walls will affect us. We pick colours to wear which reflect our personality or provide something we lack.

In the same way, when appropriate colours are directed towards the healing of the body, they penetrate the cells and energise them or dissolve negative energy. While one disease may respond to one colour, another will be affected by a different one.

For instance cancers respond to green, which is the colour of the heart centre and we need our own heart centre to be open and relaxed in order to bring this colour through effectively. People in shock or those whose minds need to be calmed respond to indigo. Someone in depression will respond favourably to the warm reds and oranges.

It is becoming recognised that colour healing is very effective. Some healers are very intuitive and send the perfect shade to help their patients. Others are not able to see different hues very clearly or are not confident that they are selecting the right ones. However, the angels of colour are always around to aid us. Whenever we think a colour and project it onto someone, an angel will support our intention. If we ask for help, then relax and allow the angels to take over, we can rest assured that they will choose the perfect colours so that the patient will get the maximum benefit.

It is counterproductive to concentrate too hard. Our task is simply to maintain a relaxed focus, so that the angels can work through us.

If we want to visualise the colour, it is always safe to focus on white light, which includes the whole range of the spectrum. The angels of healing can then choose and mix whichever shades the recipient most needs.

White is a very pure colour and when we use it for protection we are impregnable. We can be certain that the angels are very strongly with us.

I was talking about the power of white light at one of my workshops and a participant shared this story. She is very strongly clairvoyant and has always seen energy around people. At that time she had a job in a shop and once a week had to carry a considerable amount of money home. One night after work she was standing at a bus stop waiting for the bus. It was winter, already dark and she had that day's shop takings in her handbag.

In the gloom coming towards her, she saw a youth. From his energy she saw that he intended to mug her. Did she tense up and grab the bag tight as most people would do? No. She relaxed as much as she could and put white light around herself. She heard the youth's footsteps running towards her, getting nearer and nearer. Suddenly they stopped and she opened her eyes. She saw the young man's hand stretched out to grab her bag but it couldn't get through the white light. On his face was a look of indescribable horror. Then he turned and ran away as fast as he could.

When she relaxed and visualised the white light round herself, she allowed angelic protection to come to her assistance.

When I told a lawyer this story, he smiled and told me of his experience of the power of white light. He said that it was the first time he invoked it but he firmly believed it saved his life.

He was being driven by some friends on the continent. They were driving extremely fast and he felt the presence of imminent danger. He had a choice, either to go into abject terror or to trust the spiritual forces available to him. He decided to relax and protect himself with white light. Once he had done this, he sat back and knew he would be all right.

As they raced at breakneck speed down the motorway, the car in front of them had a puncture. It went all over the road but by some miracle — or by the protective power of the angels of light — missed them and their car was completely untouched.

Do we need to have trust in white light for it to work? Like everything else it follows the spiritual laws of the universe. To the exact extent that we relax and trust, the angels can come close and help us.

I firmly believe that one person's faith is stronger than the accumu-
lated doubt of many.

Celia told me that she was taken by a friend to a healing course.
They were a little late but trusted that there would be a parking space
for them. They toured round and round but couldn't find one. Finally
they came across a space in a line of cars illegally parked. Celia's friend
said, "We are doing God's work today. We can safely park here." She got
out and put white light round the car.

Celia was most agitated and upset. All morning she worried about
the car getting a parking ticket but her friend was not concerned. At
lunch time Celia wanted to go back and check that the car had not been
clamped or towed away. Her friend was bemused because she knew that
the car was protected by white angels but Celia dragged her back.

Every other car in the street had a parking ticket firmly attached to
its windscreen. Their car was untouched.

Celia was amazed. When she realised just how much worry she had
projected into the parking space, she became aware that the angels of
white light were much stronger than her negativity.

Angels are stronger than

our doubts and fears.

CHAPTER 18

Angels Of Buildings

Every house and office has an angel who looks after it. If you leave your home you can ask the angel of the building to take care of it. They will do their best to contain leaks, watch over the electrics and make sure it is safe.

If someone is sending nasty thoughts to a member of the household or a person living in the home is angry the angel will call in elementals to purify the energy or even invite Archangel Gabriel's angels of purification to shine their light in the house. Sometimes Archangel Zadkiel's angels will arrive to transmute any negative energy.

The angel of the building also keeps the elementals who live in the house contented. Because we cannot see or hear all the beings who reside in other dimensions, it does not mean they are not there, affecting our lives.

Jenny was psychic and in tune with elementals who lived in her home. The 'boss' house-spirit was very vociferous and often intimated that he would cause trouble if she wanted to make changes. She decided to enlarge a window and was talking to a friend about it, when she saw him looking very angry. That was when she realised she must communicate with him about the window and enlist his co-operation! This she did and he became helpful, charming and ensured that everything went well for the builders.

Jenny also told the angel of the building about her plan and the reason she wanted a bigger window. By doing this she transferred her vision of more light, happiness and sociability in the kitchen to the angel, who then held this expanded divine vision for the cottage. The building work went like a dream and, she told me that everyone loves to congregate in her kitchen where the sunshine pours in and they can look out over the garden.

From the moment a building is conceived in the mind of the architect or builder an angel is assigned to look after it. The quality and focus of the original concept will attract an angel of the appropriate frequency, for all things are governed by the Law of Attraction, which says that like vibrations attract each other.

Just as guardian angels hold the divine blueprint and vision for your perfect life, so the angel of a building holds the divine blueprint for its optimum use and will watch over the construction right from the digging of the foundations. The angel can only witness what the people in the house do and radiate love and light to them. It cannot interfere with their free will to do what they choose there. Prayers and visualisations will assist the guardian of the building, who can use the stream of positive energy directed towards it.

Office blocks, schools, prisons, hospitals and all buildings also have an angel to look after them. If the original intention is to build a hospital, one of Archangel Raphael's angels of healing will merge with the angel of the building, so that a healing intention is held for this place.

If enough people pray for compassion, love, peace, healing or transmutation in the hospital, additional angelic energy will merge with the angel of the hospital to help it. Thousands of angels surround healing places and, if appropriate prayers are dedicated to it, they will sing over the building and grounds to hold the energy in the light.

A nurse called Suzie worked in a hospital where the energy was very light. She told me that she always knew if a patient was going to recover because she could see the angels of healing with them. She also knew if it was their time to pass for angels would arrive to help prepare the patient for their transition. She described how one man was very unwilling to pass because he wanted to finish a film he was making but the life support was turned off. For a few minutes he was angry but when he saw the light and felt the love of the angels he was delighted to be free. She could see him laughing with wonder and joy.

When a church is consecrated the appropriate angels add their energy to the angel in charge of the structure. And if the church closes down it is de-consecrated so that the angel can freely withdraw for other work.

Wouldn't it be wonderful if there was a beautiful ceremony every time a house or any other construction was erected, dedicating it to a higher purpose. The love and joy invoked would affect the inhabitants profoundly and they would receive inspiration from the angel of the building.

Remember to make friends

with the angels of the buildings

you live in or visit.

CHAPTER 19

Angels Answer Our Prayers

Joanna confessed that she had been dreading coming for her appointment to release childhood sexual abuse. Just before her appointment she had this dream.

> *I am a native American Indian woman. I live with my partner and parents. I really love my partner and we have a very close relationship. We live in a log cabin isolated from the others. One day a civil war soldier who had gone off the rails came to the cabin. He had a big gun and kept shooting. He shot the family and the animals and then turned to me and said, "I'm going to sow my seed in you so you'll never forget me". He raped me again and again and I squeezed myself up so I couldn't become pregnant.*

I noticed that she had started by telling the dream in the present tense. Then as it became painful she disassociated from it by slipping into the past tense.

When Joanna woke from this very vivid dream, she realised it was a past life dream. She felt that all her life she had been waiting for the return of the partner who had been so cruelly killed. She told me that she had always kept men at bay and was still a virgin.

Then Joanna started to cry and said that when she was three years old, a business associate of her father's, who used to come to the house, frequently touched her genitals. She dare not tell anyone because he had told her that if she said anything he would kill her Mum and Dad.

As soon as she had told her story, angels came towards her. I watched them pulling black snakes out of her heart centre.

They indicated that she must close her eyes and go back into her childhood to the time when she was three. When she regressed to three years old again, knowing that the angels were protecting her, she was able to face the abusive man. When he threatened to kill her parents, the child laughed and called him a coward.

I directed her to bring her father into the room and tell him what had happened. She did so and was totally amazed at what unfolded as she watched. "Dad punched him", she exclaimed. "I didn't think he had it in him." For the first time in her life, she realised that he could and would defend her.

Her father turned to her and said, "You deserve to be treated with love and respect." She became aware that she had never believed she deserved to be treated well. Her Dad continued, "Now I understand why you didn't trust me. I've always felt the barrier between us."

Joanna exclaimed, "I thought that if he could let someone do that to me, then he could do it as well. Now I realise that he didn't know what was happening and that if he had known he would have defended me. My anger has gone. I didn't realise it wasn't his fault. I really feel I love him."

Then her mother came into the scene and immediately started to attack the abuser with ferocity and force. Suddenly Joanna exclaimed, "She knew. She knew something was going on."

I pointed out that sometimes we know subliminally but that's not the same as having concrete information. Joanna agreed, "Yes, she knew at some level and she told Dad to get his business out of the house." She realised that must have been hard for her unassertive mother to do this and that she had acted on her instincts and done her very best to try to help her child.

Joanna sighed and said that her anger towards her mother had all gone.

The angels started to dissolve the dark cloud of anger which had been released. As they did so, we could see that under cover of the darkness Joanna was chained to her parents — with big heavy black chains. We watched while the angels cut the chains and dissolved them in the light.

Then I was shown that Joanna's insides had been sewn up so that she could not have sex. An angel pulled out all the threads. Suddenly there were hundreds of angels standing around them singing.

Joanna's face was bright red and her eyes shining when she opened them. "I've been healed. I know I have," she said.

She told me then that she had never been able to get away from her parents although she had tried all sorts of things. Now she realised that the childhood abuse had chained her literally to the scene.

She said that before she came for the session she had prayed that the angels would come in and help her. Our prayers are always answered.

56

I spoke to Joanna a couple of months later. She said to me, "I feel whole for the first time in my life. I feel that I am no longer looking for love, support and protection outside myself." Then she added. "Before, I knew that intellectually, but now I feel it inside. I've got more confidence and self-worth. I can't think of a better way to put it than that I feel whole."

Thank you angels.

Our prayers for the highest good

are always answered

CHAPTER 20

Angels Of Love

Sometimes we can be very caring and spiritual people and yet have ill-nesses or disabilities for which we can find no cause in this life. Larry was one such young man. He worked only intermittently because of a bad back and permanent tiredness.

When I directed his unconscious mind to take him to the source of his problem, he found himself as a newborn baby full of hate.

He must have carried unresolved hatred in his soul which he had brought into this life. Naturally it affected his relationships, his life's journey and his health.

With a visualisation I helped him open his heart centre and held the energy while angels came into the room and in their infinite love and mercy pulled the dark hatred from his heart. Then they filled his heart with light and peace.

He phoned a few days later to say how incredibly different he felt.

The angels of love are pure white. They often travel with archangels and angels and are radiating love into every corner. Often they just wait somewhere holding the energy of divine love at that place. Frequently they travel very fast to help people or animals. Because they are such high frequency beings they touch you with healing as they pass.

Since I have been looking at Orbs, the light body of angels, on film I have been intrigued to see several instances where the photographer has asked the angels for a message from a loved one in spirit. In response angels of love had formed themselves into a clear heart shape on the photograph – an unmistakeable message

We are so afraid of our darkness that we often deny it. A young lady, Pauline, who had done a great deal of personal growth work came to me with a jealousy problem, which is always about not feeling good enough.

I asked if she had sought the past life cause of her jealousy and she said she had experienced several regressions. They had all helped to scrape away some of the problem but none had cleared out the darkness.

I had a feeling that this session might be different because a very beautiful angel had come into the room with her and was making itself visible to me. It was hovering above her with its hands in a praying position and I knew that we must ask for grace to release the blockage.

The angel showed me a door in the young lady's mind, fastened with rusty bolts and a similar one in her heart! I was being shown that the darkness which caused her to feel so bad was locked into her heart and mind. She felt so unworthy that she constantly expected her partners to find someone else better.

When I regressed her she discovered that in another life she had been a light soul born to a mother who was a black witch, filled with hatred. Instead of bringing light into this family of darkness, which had been her intention when she chose that challenging life, she allowed the terrible darkness to fill her. She felt consumed with black rage and hatred of all people and life itself.

Her beautiful angel, radiating gold, deep blue and pink, now put its hands into her chest and round her heart. Pauline and I could both see the blackness, like an octopus clinging to her heart, with its huge tentacles spreading through her body.

I expected the angel to take the octopus and dissolve it in the light. Instead it very gently and lovingly lifted it from Pauline's heart, stroked it and took it away for healing. Then the angel came back and lifted Pauline's heart out of her body and took it for cleansing and purification in a beautiful waterfall.

When her heart was returned to her body, I presumed that would be the end but no. The angel brought back the octopus transformed through divine love into something pink. Pauline saw a rose quartz crystal. We put the crystal into her heart and by now she was glowing.

When she opened her eyes at the end of the session she said she felt that something really deep had taken place. She knew there had been a major change within her.

Angels, with their infinite

love and compassion,

are waiting to help us.

CHAPTER 21

Earth Angels

There have always been reports of people arriving from nowhere and helping others, then disappearing. Many believe these to be angels, using human guise.

A friend of mine wrote me this note about his conversation with a lovely, really sprightly lady in her 70s.

> *She told me that she was at Victoria coach station looking for a coach to Gatwick, and realised that she would not make it in time. She stood with her baggage and prayed for help, and a little black man appeared by her and said that he could help her. He was sent by God, he said, and took her and her baggage to the BA check in at the railway station, and put her on the train in plenty of time to catch her flight. She is convinced that he was an angel.*

I was told the following story by a friend, who has had a very special and charmed life. She believes that an Earth angel helped her even before she was born. At that time her mother was eight months pregnant with her and certainly was not anticipating her imminent arrival.

The family lived in a small village in the country where everyone knew everyone else. Her mother was scrubbing the front door step when a stranger appeared at the front gate and told her to send for her husband and doctor and to go and lie down immediately. The baby was about to be born.

Such was the command in the stranger's voice that her mother unquestioningly did what she was told. Her husband came home quickly. The doctor arrived and the baby was born within the hour. Upon enquiry round the village, no one had seen a stranger that morning.

Earth angels appear and then disappear
when their task is accomplished.

Recently I was sent a letter with this extraordinary story from Patricia O'Flaherty.

> *In 1980, in October, we moved as a family to Norway in connection with my (now ex) husband's work. The children were eight and six respectively. It was a tremendous upheaval. We'd had three weeks notice. I'd had to give up my job, pack up the house, organise 1001 things and had had little sleep and a lot of anxiety. We arrived in Oslo by car after a twenty-four hour ferry journey and a long drive through Sweden and southern Norway and finally booked into the Grand Hotel where we were to stay for two weeks whilst we found accommodation.*
>
> *The first day or two we collapsed and slept and ventured out on short trips as a family in the car. But on Monday morning my husband went to work and the children were feeling perky and energetic. I felt awful: sick, muzzy headed, shaky and exhausted but after lunch we decided to have a little wander to explore the city.*
>
> *We set off. I hadn't intended to go far but somehow we seemed to get further and further away from the shops. The day got darker and darker. Cars were driving with their lights on. It was bitterly cold and suddenly we were lost somewhere under a motorway flyover.*
>
> *I felt panic stricken. The children were tired. There was no-one about and I thought I might faint, I was feeling so peculiar. I remember asking for help from the bottom of my heart. There was no way I could get out of this pickle myself.*
>
> *Suddenly, a tall, fair man in a raincoat appeared from somewhere. I didn't notice where. He understood English perfectly and smilingly, kindly, started to escort us. The rest of the journey is like a dream that one has. Suffice to say, I "came to" at the kiosk on the corner by the Grand Hotel.*
>
> *I have no explanation for what happened but am convinced it was an angel helping us home.*

If a child is whining and whingeing without really trying, we tend to ignore him. But if the child is in genuine trouble or despair, we naturally rush to his assistance. We are God's children and I believe that when we are in real need, God sends a person or an angel to help us.

This has happened to me in many ways big and small since my very first cry for help was answered by the being of light. I think I was such a long way down the pit of despondency that I needed a lot of help to get out of it.

A year or so after that first experience, I was still feeling very frightened and alone. I went to a lecture. I sat at the front of the hall and have to confess I couldn't concentrate on the talk, as I was so entrenched in my own survival fears. After the lecture a stranger came up to me from the back of the hall. He apologised for tuning into my thoughts during the talk but he wanted to tell me that everything would be all right. I must not worry for I was being guided and protected.

A week later a stranger came up to me in the street and gave me an almost identical message. I do not imagine these were angels but I expect they were prompted by angelic beings to give me these messages of hope.

On a third occasion I was feeling very low. Something made me look up into the sky. I saw huge upturned hands filling the sky as if to say. We will hold you. I could hardly believe what I saw but it encouraged me greatly.

Earth angels come to help,

encourage and support us.

CHAPTER 22

Practical Angels

There are myriads of angels ready and willing to help human souls. We only have to ask and they are there bringing us what we need.

Lots of people know about the angel of parking spaces. When we ask for a parking angel and tell him where we want to park, he will do his utmost to clear the space for us. It is the same with the angel of traffic lights. Ask your angel to turn them green as quickly as possible to facilitate your journey.

A friend visiting from Canada told me that he always asked his driving angel to protect him from speed traps and cameras when in the car. He said it worked amazingly. He would do nothing consciously but would find that his speed had automatically slowed down and he would hear of others being fined at that spot on that day. A number of people have written to me to say that I must remove this story as speed kills. One understandably angry lady told me that her sister was killed by a driver who was travelling too fast and I felt tremendous compassion for her.

To our Earth perception this is a terrible tragedy but the angels remind us that the soul chooses the method of passing and that no one dies unless it is their time. I do not advocate reckless driving nor the removal of speed limits. Of course we all need to drive with consideration, caution and care. However, there is a wider perspective. Your guardian angel will keep you safe if it is not your time to pass or to experience the lessons offered by an accident.

Another lady on a workshop had us all in fits of laughter when she shared how she always invited an angel to help with the housework. Before she started to vacuum the house she would invite in her vacuuming angel and the chore would be done in half the normal time, easily and lightly. When the washing machine broke down and there was a huge pile of washing to be done by hand, she said, "It was no trouble. I asked the washing angel to help and the whole lot was done in two hours and I felt wonderful." It seems they give us energy as they help.

Angels are so full of delight. They help us lightly with shopping, typing, accounts, literally anything we want. Isn't it wonderful to think that when we are struggling to balance the books, there is an accounting angel hovering above the computer waiting to make it all easy. When we are agonising over which present to buy, there is a shopping angel longing to point us towards the perfect gift!

We do make life difficult for ourselves...and there are all those angels just waiting to smooth the way for us as long as our intentions are pure or we hand over to divine right timing. I am an impatient person who likes things done immediately. The danger of this is that I make snap decisions without always listening to my angelic guidance. I get things done but sometimes have an impression of my angel shaking its head in despair!

Recently I was co-writing a booklet and we used the printing firm recommended by someone, who was not doing such spiritual work. Everything was delayed. For six weeks in succession the company promised us the finished goods. Each week at the last minute something went wrong and they did not arrive. Eventually I asked the angels. They said that the work was being printed in Lithuania where the workers were not happy and this was affecting our project which was highly spiritual. They also gave us an exercise to do which breathed Christ light into the publication. We could literally feel this raising the energy of all concerned.

The angels told us that they had not speeded up the printing because they wanted the booklet to be released when there was a new wave of cosmic energy.

The week by week delays pressed all my buttons and I felt furious with the printers. A tug of war arose within me for I know that sending rage to anyone is counterproductive as it always comes back to the sender in some form. Equally I am very aware that blessing the person who has wronged you dissolves your anger, changes their energy too and helps the entire situation. How difficult this is! Each week as the printers made yet another human error I would watch my angry thoughts erupt. Then I would dissolve them in gold light and ask the angels to bless the printers with self worth, confidence and efficiency. I visualised them happy and at peace. I am sure I got angelic brownie points for trying but was a long way from feeling true oneness with them!

As well as guardian angels, there are angels of mercy, truth, love, compassion, humility, peace and every conceivable quality. When we live at higher levels of consciousness we pray for qualities rather than things. Spiritual Law says that whatever we focus on increases. So when we focus on a quality such as love or peace an angel helps bring more of this higher frequency quality into our lives.

Of course, the same is true of the base qualities. If we focus on fear, greed, lust or any negative quality the dark forces will direct more of these feelings and events into our lives.

However angels bring hope. They try to inspire and comfort us in times of trouble. Sometimes we feel too down to feel their presence even though they are trying to lift us. Then, if it is karmically permitted, they will inspire someone to lighten us.

My son, Justin, tells a delightful story about an incident he witnessed on the underground. The train was fairly crowded and there was one woman in the compartment who was glowering at everyone. She looked so unhappy and forbidding that the atmosphere in the compartment was getting heavier and heavier. When the train stopped, a young man got in. He sat down and pulled two very long thin balloons out of his pocket, one red and one green.

Everyone was watching as he blew them up. He proceeded to twist the balloons together until he had fashioned a red rose. At the next station he got up and presented the rose to the glowering lady. Then he jumped off the train. Suddenly she was beaming from ear to ear as she held the balloon rose. Justin found himself smiling broadly as he watched. He looked round and everyone was grinning and laughing with pleasure.

Angels bring light

to the heaviest tasks and

darkest situations.

CHAPTER 23

Angels Help A Marriage

Serena was a young and attractive married woman with small children. Her looks belied an inner turmoil. She was so angry with her husband, who could not support her financially and emotionally, that she had refused to have sex with him for several years. She was contemplating living with him in this celibate way until the children were older because she could not bear the thought of him touching her.

I talked with her for some time helping her to become more aware of her patterns and then she agreed to relax and invite the angels in to help her.

As soon as the angels came closer, they moved to her heart and showed me that her heart was very bruised emotionally. They stroked and soothed her damaged heart until it was mended.

Then they moved down to her solar plexus. It was like a dusty cellar full of old memories and they worked hard to clear out all the rubbish and take it to the light where it was dissolved. When they had cleared out and cleansed and blessed her solar plexus I asked her to imagine her husband in front of her.

"Oh, I'm surrounded in black and he's all black and red," she said. Black and red together are the colours of imminent explosion. He was clearly at the end of his tether.

The angels took a long time gently washing away all the dark angry energy around both of them and dissolved the cords which entangled them.

When they had done this, Serena said to me, "We are holding hands and supporting each other and we share our body fluids." I was quite surprised at this. However, I merely asked the angels if they would continue to bring both of them together.

She returned for another appointment two weeks later and I was delighted at the vibrant and glowing woman who walked in. She said that after the help from the angels she had gone home feeling totally different. She and her husband had a night of passion.

Next day she felt a bit angry and scared but that passed and now they were loving and close to each other and making love again. She said, "I can now clearly see how I can make things work, not what he has to do. I am clear about where I am going with my work and realise we can now be joint providers. For the first time I feel quite comfortable with that."

She added that a friend, who was staying with them, had stayed with them four months earlier and was astonished at the difference in their relationship — she could hardly believe it.

We live in the physical planes but our spirits also move in other planes, the emotional or astral, mental or spiritual ones. However, our experiences while out of the body in spirit profoundly affect what happens to our physical life. A couple with three young children were becoming increasingly unhappy with each other. She was very angry with him for many reasons. Her husband, who I will call Jack, felt she was unreasonably angry and did not know how to cope with it for he did not really know what was wrong. I asked the angels what the underlying reason for her anger was and they told me that the husband was having an affair in the astral planes at night. She was unconsciously picking this up. I asked if he knew what he was doing and they said, no he was completely unaware.

The next time I saw Jack I told him all this and he was totally bemused and felt helpless because he did not know what to do. I suggested that he uncord himself from this woman on the astral planes and make a decree that no matter what he now totally released her and would never have any contact with her again. He agreed to do this.

Two weeks later he reported that their relationship had improved immeasurably. I saw his wife and was delighted that her anger had evaporated and she was radiating an aura of peace. I realised that she had psychically sensed the change that had taken place in the inner planes.

When we allow them to,

angels will do their best

to bring two partners

in a marriage together.

CHAPTER 24

Interdimensional Portals

All the mountains, rivers, rocks, gardens or trees have their own angel to guard them and to direct the elementals who work within them.

When we have a sense of the power of a mountain or of a waterfall, we are in tune with the angel who is guarding that place.

There are power spots on planet Earth to which people are drawn because they feel peaceful or relaxed when they are there. Usually these are places of great natural beauty which induce a sense of wonder and awe. When I look at pictures of such places I am surprised at the number of guardian angel Orbs that collect there. The angels said that guardian angels often go to these high energy places to collect prana to take it back to the person they are looking after. Their service work is limitless.

Some of these power spots are interdimensional portals through which humans and beings in other dimensions can communicate more easily. Visiting one of these gateways opens us to impressions, visions, intuitive flashes and any form of spiritual or psychic message.

A great many of the interdimensional portals are one-way; in other words, the spiritual beings can come through the vortex to communicate with us. A few of them are two-way and through these we can receive universal messages as well as transmit out into the universe. Stonehenge in England is one such two-way communication centre, which has been re-opened at this moment in time. The most powerful of the two way interdimensional portals on planet Earth is Machu Picchu in Peru. There is also one in Tibet and another at the Great Zimbabwe in Africa.

The only entry aliens have to our planet is through these portals. Even angels find it easier to use these open gateways to access Earth. However, if we do not protect these, our precious entry points, dark angels and negative aliens can come through.

Originally these portals were most sacred and holy places, looked after with ceremony and love by specially trained initiates. Over the past few thousand years we have neglected to protect and put light into them, with disastrous results for Earth.

A few years ago I went to Machu Picchu with friends. While there we had terrible nightmares, which we were told on return, were the dark forces attacking us. Nevertheless, we were informed that the area drank in the light we took with us like parched earth responding to gentle rain. Certainly meditating and ohm-ing at Machu Picchu was the highlight of the trip for me.

When humans of high intention and spiritual focus visit or think about Stonehenge, Machu Picchu and other portals their light automatically helps to protect these important gateways. We can also pour love and light energy out into the universe through them.

The mighty Thoth who was a High Priest in the golden age of Atlantis and later became a God in Egypt, is guardian of the portal at Machu Picchu. He allows through the turquoise angels of communication and their helpers, who form the crop circles. Crop circles are symbols, which are keys that unlock universal information within our minds. We do not need consciously to decode each symbol for the messages work subliminally.

In 1996 a huge crop circle was formed opposite Stonehenge. I was told that it was placed there to increase the energy of that portal. The coded message of the symbol invited people to go through the portal in their dream states and travel intergalactically, so that they could learn about the vastness of the universe. This would expand their consciousness.

Whenever people sit in a genuine crop circle they connect with the angels.

Many of the evil forces have been able to draw near over the last few thousand years because of our neglect of the sacred protection rituals and the sheer amount of negativity and fear that humans on planet Earth emit. This feeds the consciousness of the dark angels and keeps them alive and active on the planet. However, if you remain positive, loving and light they cannot influence or touch you in any way.

All those who promote war are listening to dark angels. Angels of light always whisper of peace.

The many light beings and angels, who so much want to approach and work with us, need a love vibration from us in order to be able to come closer. Our loving energy also provides nourishment for them. They need to be loved and cherished as much as we do. When we project love, gratitude and other high vibrations out through the portals into the Universe, we send an invitation for the spiritual realms to come to us.

It is imperative at this time when the consciousness of planet Earth is shifting that we send light along the ley lines to the pyramids, from where it connects to the other planets and galaxies.

We can also send light through the interdimensional portals to the cosmic energy lines which link to other planets. In this way Earth can be realigned and take its rightful place in the universe once more. Naturally it helps if we send out as much love and light as we can at all times. However, when we project through the portals our intention goes further out into the universe where highly evolved light beings, such as the Universal angel Butyalil, can respond. The angels will direct our beams of love and light to the best possible place.

I am delighted to say that so much light has now been radiated by humanity into the universe that unicorns have responded by returning to Earth for the first time since the fall of Atlantis. Unicorns are seventh dimensional beings of the angelic realms, who help to bring about the longings of our souls.

Light contains spiritual knowledge and information. Darkness is absence of light and being in the dark literally means having no spiritual understanding. Power spots are good places to visit if we wish to open up more quickly to the universal wisdom that is available.

By sending out love and light

you can help Earth take its

rightful place in the Universe.

CHAPTER 25

Angels And The Nature Kingdoms

Angels are guardians of the natural world. They lovingly assist humans and the nature kingdoms to evolve. They direct the elementals who tend nature. These are the fairies, elves, imps, gnomes, sylphs, salamanders, pixies and fauns among others. No one ever works alone on Earth. Angelic beings called gemllia, who vibrate at a faster frequency than guardian angels, look after the elementals.

Where elementals live in close proximity to humans, they are affected by our emotions. It works like this. Salamanders, the fire elementals, help fires to burn. When we are gathered round a cheerful blaze, the salamanders are merrily at work. If humans are angry and out of harmony, salamanders can respond by creating havoc with fire. If a house or neighbourhood burns down, the salamanders are sparked by the — often suppressed — chaotic emotions of the people who live there.

Fire is also a cleanser. When people are cremated, the salamanders help with the release of old family patterns, negative habits and thought forms which might otherwise attach to vulnerable members of the family who are still alive.

If there is much negativity in a country, which needs to be transmuted, fire is one of the elements which may be used to clear the old. When a huge amount of fear or anger is projected onto a forest fire for example, the elementals will absorb it and the fire will become out of control.

These big conflagrations are now shown on television so you have the opportunity to send thoughts of calm to the salamanders and also ask the angels of peace and transmutation to help the area.

I was told this delightful story by Pamela Russell of Evesham who used to own a soft furnishings shop, which was in a small cottage in an old listed building.

Before she bought it an elderly lady had lived there for many years until she had gone into a home and eventually died. The old lady had been very fond of her home and her presence was frequently felt. She was also quite mischievous. Pamela would leave her favourite thimble with her work and it would sometimes just disappear. Everyone would hunt for it. Then they would firmly tell the spirit of the old lady to return it and next morning it would be sitting in the middle of the table! Apparently this only happened when a new employee came to work there. It was as if the old lady's ghost wanted to know who had come into her home and be acknowledged by that person. Until she received attention and acknowledgement she made her presence felt with her tricks. Once she had got to know the newcomer and in turn been accepted by her, she stopped hiding the thimble.

Whenever the thimble vanished or they sensed her presence, there would be a lovely smell of flowers in the room. They could smell stocks, lilies of the valley and sweet peas. The old lady's daughter-in-law told Pamela that, when she was alive, her mother-in-law used to make bouquets of flowers and wreaths from old fashioned scented garden flowers.

Then one day there was a fire in the shop. After the mess was cleared up and the shop repainted the old lady never came back. I suspect the fire elementals cleansed the old memories away, so that the old lady was no longer attached to her home and decided to move on to the light.

The air spirits are sylphs, tinier than a humming bird. Their main task is to bring the light of the sun into the leaves of flowers and plants. They also keep the air round flowers pure, which is why people breathe more freely when out in nature. I have often taken a deep breath when I am near a vase of flowers and it is not just for the perfume. Unconsciously I must have realised that the air by the flowers was clearer. Sylphs also assist the flight of birds.

I was watching a big fat fluffy blackbird baby being fed by its parents. When I went outside the parent birds flew away and abandoned the little one. It tried to fly but could not so I felt I had to stay outside in case a cat jumped over the fence. The little bird hopped into a corner and I was not sure what to do until I thought of the sylphs. The next time it flapped its wings I asked the sylphs to be the air under them to help it fly. It worked! The little bird flew onto the fence and then onto the branch of a tree. With a grateful sigh of relief I was at last able to go inside and cook the dinner.

Sylphs smile in the gentle breeze of summer or they can be whipped up into frenzied tornados or hurricanes. Like all elementals they link into our suppressed anger and express it for us as violent wind conditions. In doing so, they blow the mental, emotional and psychic cobwebs away.

When someone says they are going to brave the elements, they literally mean they are going to brave the elemental energy of air, water, fire or earth which is being released.

Fairies too are air elementals. They are very pure and innocent and take care of flowers. Where we garden organically and they feel safe and loved, fairies will help flowers and vegetables to grow. I know many people who have seen fairies or have them living in their gardens or even window boxes. I know I have many fairies in my garden because fairy Orbs appear in many of my photographs. They are like pinpricks of bright light. However I have only ever once seen a fairy myself and that was at the Findhorn Foundation, the huge spiritual community in Scotland. They are renowned for their wonderful produce, which is grown in attunement with nature and here the veil between the worlds is very thin.

Seeing that fairy was an experience I shall never forget. I was listening to a talk. In the middle of the room was a bowl of catmint flowers with a candle in the centre of it. (Catmint leaves are silver but the flowers are a beautiful mauveish blue.) To my surprise and delight I saw a brilliant light, the exact colour of the flowers, hovering above the vase. It was about 1ft or 30cms tall and I realised it was a fairy, looking exactly like Tinkerbell from the Peter Pan books I loved in childhood, only shimmering, shining and luminous in a way I would not have expected. I watched it move above and around the flowers. Even when I looked away and back again it was still there. It was much more enthralling than the lecture but eventually I had to focus on the work again and the beautiful fairy disappeared from my sight.

I always used to think that fairies were sweet little elementals. Now I know that fairies are underestimated. They are mighty, powerful beings who work with the unicorns and angels to hold the energy on Earth.

There are angels in charge of groups of fairies.

Undines, who are water sprites, and mermaids, tend plants under the sea. The psychic sailors of old occasionally saw mermaids and were bewitched by their innocence, purity, essence of fun and light.

Gnomes are earth elementals, who work with stones, minerals and jewels deep in the Earth. One winter evening a friend was arriving after dark and when he walked up the path I took some photos to see if there were any angel Orbs about. To my surprise there was a huge angel of love radiating out Archangel Michael's blue protective energy into the hedge. I asked the angels why it was there and was told that it was protecting some gnomes who were sheltering there. Why did they need protection, I asked? The angel Orb was protecting the gnomes from us humans, not because we would harm them but because our vibration was so different.

Interestingly I often photograph huge angels of love with Archangel Michael in a pine tree in my garden, where fairies, pixies and elves reside. It is lovely to think that the angels are looking after their little brothers and sisters in this way.

There are two parallel streams of evolution. One is the angelic stream. The young ones of this stream are the elementals, who eventually evolve into angels through the various orders, overseen by the Lords of Karma and, ultimately, by Source.

The other evolutionary thread is that along which animals and humans evolve. Vibrating at a faster frequency than humans are the spirit guides under the direction of the Ascended Masters, again answerable to Source.

When we honour the natural world,

we help the angels

and according to spiritual law

we in turn receive help.

CHAPTER 26

The Archangels
And Universal Angels

There are millions of archangels who work throughout the universe. They are in charge of great projects for the light and look after the ranks of angels below them. Only a few archangels connect with humans on Earth, though more are now doing so.

The most well known are Archangels Michael, Gabriel, Uriel, Raphael and Metatron. The angel of death, Archangel Azriel is also well recognised, though often not by name.

Others have been assisting us quietly behind the scenes, such as Archangels Chamuel, Jophiel and Sandalphon, Christiel and Mariel. They each have individual divine energies and their own special tasks and they help with the spiritual development of human chakras, preparing us for ascension.

New archangels are now being assigned to Earth or are ready to work with humans. One of these is Archangel Purlimiek who is in charge of nature. Archangel Fhelyai looks after the animal kingdom. Archangel Butyalil, the universal angel is in charge of the stars and cosmic currents and Archangel Gersisa, of the inner Earth, works with the ley lines.

Each archangel has a twin flame. Because we have been a male orientated planet we tend to honour the one of the pair which carries the masculine energy. Now, at last the divine feminine is starting to return, so that the feminine aspects are coming forward to touch us with their wisdom and gentleness.

Each archangel has a retreat location in the etheric around planet Earth. We can ask at night before we go to sleep to be taken to one of these retreats for purification, a strengthening of our qualities and any assistance we may need.

~ Archangels Metatron and Sandalphon ~

Metatron is the mightiest of the mighty. He is known as the servant of God, the Heavenly Scribe who transmits the daily orders of Source to all the archangels. He is very linked to Egypt, Atlantis and Lemuria when he was helping the planet and the people to reach their highest potential. He brought through Sacred Geometry from Source and used his wisdom to overlight the building of the pyramids so that their message resonates out in the universes.

A big part of his spiritual work is to help Earth connect to other planets, so he holds the energy between planets. He was one of the angels that led the people of Israel out of the wilderness after their exodus from Egypt. He also overlit and channelled through Enoch the scribe who was a pious man and wise leader of his people.

He is working with those who are opening up to their ascension pathways, so he is in charge of the development of the stellar gateway chakra, the twelfth chakra, which is the highest frequency spiritual energy centre that a human can develop and is high above the crown. If you imagine a golden ladder to Source, he is helping people to take the final step.

He radiates the qualities of commitment, wisdom and discipline, so when you are dedicated to your spiritual path and disciplined on your journey, he will come into and add his energy to your life, whether you can see him or not.

When many people tune in to send a mass healing, Metatron orchestrates it. He synchronises the energy to go in divine right timing. He switches the light on when everyone is in place. An example of this is Angel Awareness Day, organised by the Diana Cooper School, when groups all over the world send out the light. It is a massive opportunity for change on the planet and Metatron helps to optimize this.

He is working with the ascension of the planet.

No one can step onto the ascension ladder unless the earth star chakra, which is below the feet, is operational. That chakra is governed by Archangel Metatron's twin flame, Archangel Sandalphon. It is the supreme example of how the masculine and feminine are equally important, balancing energies.

Archangel Metatron, carrying the masculine energy, is the only archangel allowed to look directly into God's light, which is why he is sometimes called the Prince of the Countenance.

Archangel Sandalphon carries the feminine energy and helps you connect deeply into Mother Earth. He is known as 'He who wears sandals before God,' because he collects and delivers the prayers of humanity up to Source. He is also the angel of music and is called the tall angel because he bridges Earth and heaven. Strangely he is referred to as 'He' even though he carries the feminine energy.

Archangel Metatron vibrates on a colour frequency from deep gold to orange and even red, like the light of the sun. Archangel Sandalphon's colour is black and white, as the yin yang symbol. Black is the extreme feminine vibration. Imagine a dark, mysterious cave or womb, where new ideas gestate and deep connection is made to the divine. The white is the light, containing spiritual information and knowledge, which wakes up the seeds and helps them to grow.

Archangel Metatron's retreat is at Luxor, Egypt. That of Archangel Sandalphon is at the magical crystal cave in Guatemala. Both of these are important Ascension Retreats. You can ask to visit them in your meditations or while asleep for teaching and energy which will accelerate your ascension.

When Kathy Crosswell and I were writing *Enlightenment and Ascension Through Orbs* we were sent several magnificent Orbs of Archangel Metatron. In each case he had a pure white angel of love with him. I started asking him to come into my Orb pictures and photographed two of his angels, but both were very small. Then one evening in the back garden, he appeared as a glorious Orb with Archangel Jophiel, the angel of wisdom, and an angel of love. Since then I have been very aware of his presence.

~ Archangels Michael and Faith ~

Archangel Michael is probably the best known and loved of all the archangels for he is the warrior and protector who looks after you. He places his deep blue cloak of protection round you to keep you safe when your spirit travels at night and he also physically and psychically protects you during the day.

He is one of the three angels mentioned in the Bible and his name means, 'One who is like God'. Archangel Michael's retreat is at Banff in Alberta, Canada.

Jody asked Archangel Michael to protect her journey when she was taking her children to school by car. Suddenly she had a funny feeling she should take a different route from usual. 'I don't know why!' she said. 'I just had this impression I must go on the scenic route even though it takes longer. The kids moaned but I did it thankfully.' There was a multiple pile up on the main road which she would most certainly have been caught up in. It really deepened her faith in Archangel Michael.

As I wrote those last words I realised Michael had probably been directing my fingers for his twin flame is Archangel Faith and I had just typed the word faith in that last sentence. She carries the feminine energy and her task is to increase your faith and trust in life and in yourself. Faith is one of the most powerful energies there is on Earth. It guarantees success and draws forth mighty rewards from the Almighty.

One of my angel teachers in South Africa loves Archangel Michael. She told me this story in her slow, deep voice. She lived in a township where people were envious of her because she ran a thriving home for disabled people. One jealous person paid a man to break into her home and trash it. The first she knew of it was a phone call from the would-be assailant saying, 'I was paid to do this job. I have been five times to this house to do the job. Every single time there is a huge soldier dressed in blue holding a sword blocking my way!' He paused and she could sense him shaking his head in disbelief. 'Tell me! Where can I get such muti (magic) for myself?'

Archangel Michael is in charge of the angels of protection. I was waiting for friends to answer their door one evening. As I stood on their doorstep I took a few random photographs. One of them captured two huge angels of protection Orbs in front of the house opposite. My friend told me that was her doctor's surgery and there had been a number of burglaries recently in the area. Clearly the angels were on duty making sure his house was safe.

Eva Sofie e-mailed me about her experience with Archangel Michael.

'I would like to share a story with you that came back to me when I read about the archangels on your website. It happened a few years ago in the south of Sweden. I had borrowed a friend's summerhouse for a few days. I needed to get away and study, I had an exam coming up. The first night I started feeling very frightened in the house, though I am normally not afraid of the dark. I could not sleep at all, it was so scary. During the next day it was nearly ok. The following night it became even worse and I was lying in bed stiff and scared and did not dare to move. I asked for help and protection. After a while a huge angel with blue wings came down towards me and he put his soft wings around me and I fell asleep at once.

The following morning I packed and went home. I thanked
the angel for protecting me. I learnt afterwards that a very
bitter and sick man had lived and died in the house and he
obviously did not want me there!
It was a wonderful experience to meet with Archangel
Michael!'

Ask for help and Archangel Michael will protect you.

~ Archangels Gabriel and Hope ~

Archangel Gabriel, whose name means 'Hero of God' or 'God is my Strength', is one of the three archangels mentioned in the Bible and he vibrates on pure white light.

In Islam the angels are guided by Archangel Gabriel, who dictated the Koran to Mohammed and the Sufis of the Islamic mystery schools are strongly connected to angels.

The etheric retreat of Archangel Gabriel is at Mount Shasta, Northern California, set in the Rocky Mountains and one of the most beautiful locations in the world. I have been there several times and always feel the energy of Archangel Gabriel as well as that of the Masters, especially St. Germain.

On one occasion I was in a car with two friends. We turned a corner and there ahead of us was Mount Shasta itself, glowing white with snow. Illuminated in it was the face of Jesus the Christ! We all saw it and without hesitation the driver stopped and we jumped out to stare at it in awe. It lasted a full five minutes, then a cloud shaped like a bird floated across it and the vision disappeared.

I often ask to go to Archangel Gabriel's retreat for purification while I am asleep, for this is something that is essential on the ascension pathway. In addition if you want clarity about your next step or about some decision you have to make ask to be taken to this retreat while you dream.

Whenever a person or place needs purification many of Archangel Gabriel's angels arrive, shining white light to raise the frequency.

They will also bring us clarity if we can't make a decision. Claire did not know what she wanted to do next with her life. There were so many options and she felt very bemused and muddled. She decided to sit down for half an hour every day for a week, invoke Archangel Gabriel and ask for clarity about her next step. By the third day she thought she was wasting her time as her future seemed a tangled mess, but she persisted. By the fifth day some of the strands of her future seemed to have sorted themselves out. On the seventh day, she was totally clear about her decisions, which were major. She let go of her boy friend and decided to move to another town and train to become an alternative practitioner. 'Archangel Gabriel gave me the clarity I needed,' she told me, 'And I have never regretted it.'

I always sense Archangel Hope, the feminine energy, as a rainbow of light. She is an energy full of compassion and she visits those who are depressed or have lost their way in order to bring them hope and expectation again. She will help your aspirations and purify your visions.

~ Archangels Raphael and Mary ~

Raphael meaning 'God has Healed' is the third archangel mentioned in the Bible. All archangels can heal but Archangel Raphael is known as the healing angel for that is his special focus. Invoke him when you want to receive or give healing. He works on the emerald green vibration, the colour of balance.

Archangel Raphael is in charge of the development of the third eye chakra and is the patron saint of the blind because he enhances inner sight. He is also connected with abundance for when you control your thoughts and focus on the positive you have the power to draw in the abundance you desire.

This is the biblical story of Archangel Raphael coming down to Earth disguised as a human being to help the good in response to their prayers.

> *Tobit was a good man who helped the poor and disadvantaged. One night he was blinded and could no longer work, so he and his family became very poor. He prayed for help.*
>
> *At the same time in another town a good woman, called Sarah was having an unbelievably difficult time. She had married seven times and each time her new groom was found dead in the morning! No one knew why this should be so but the devil had killed them. So poor Sarah still had to live with her parents and no one wanted to marry her. She too prayed for help.*

Tobit and Sarah's prayers reached God and Archangel Raphael was despatched to Earth in human disguise to help them. God reminded Tobit that he was owed silver by his cousin, who was Sarah's father. The money would greatly help his financial situation. God also impressed upon Tobit that his son Tobias could travel to the distant town to fetch it.

Archangel Raphael took on the role of a camel driver, who was hired by Tobias to take him across the desert to fetch the silver. On the way Tobias went to wash in a wide river. A glittering fish jumped out of the water and Raphael told him to keep its liver, heart and gall bladder in little sealed pots.

When they eventually reached Sarah's family, her father not only handed over the silver but asked Tobias to marry his daughter. Tobias did not want to be the eighth dead husband, so he asked his servant for advice. Raphael suggested he marry the girl and told him to use specific psychic protection — burning the heart and liver of the fish.

The marriage took place. Throughout the wedding night Tobias fed the fire and burnt the heart and liver of the fish as suggested by Raphael. When the devil entered, he was repelled by the smell of the burning offal so that he could not harm Tobias. Then Raphael chased and overcame him.

The young couple journeyed back across the desert to Tobias's family home. Before he met his father again, Raphael told Tobias how to heal the old man's blindness using the gall of the fish. When the father's sight returned, he recognised Raphael as an angel. Raphael then disappeared.

Peter, a friend of a friend, died of cancer. He was a very genuine and giving person and much loved. He had always said he would come back and give a message as soon as possible but I was surprised he managed to get through so quickly to his friends. He said that he was very happy and loving it in the light. He added that he was being held in Archangel Raphael's light while the cancer was healed from his essence.

Archangel Raphael's retreat is in Fatima Portugal while Mary's is in Lourdes, both places renowned for healing.

Call on Archangel Raphael for all kinds of healing.

~ Mary ~

Mary is a universal angel, in a much faster frequency band than her twin flame Raphael. She overlit the mother of Jesus, who took her name.

Mary's angels are full of compassion and healing energy. Call on Mary if you wish to help someone who has passed over. Her angels will find them and make sure they are helped to the light.

If a small child or baby needs help Mother Mary has the perfect divine feminine vibration to heal or support them. She responds to calls from the hearts of all mothers.

Irene had a young baby who was very ill in hospital. She called me in desperation and I said I would light a candle for the child and ask Mother Mary to look after her. At the same time Irene phoned her friends and asked them all to invoke Mother Mary to bring healing to her baby. Then she went straight back to the hospital. As she entered the intensive care unit she saw a flash of beautiful blue coming from the cot. The nurse was smiling and said the baby had turned the corner and was going to be alright.

If a baby or child needs help or healing surround it in Mother Mary blue and invoke her assistance.

~ Archangels Uriel and Aurora ~

Uriel's name means 'Fire of God' and it is Archangel Uriel who gave the Kabbalah, the Hebrew mystic tradition, to humanity. He is also said to have warned Noah of the impending flood. Archangel Uriel's retreat is in the Tatra Mountains, south of Cracow, Poland.

He is in charge of the development of the solar plexus chakra, which is where people store their fears as well as their inability to digest life or assimilate experiences. Here much past life wisdom is also retained. This chakra is a huge psychic pump which checks how safe you or your loved ones are. Feelers go from here to make sure your child, friend or partner is okay. If all is not well you have a gut feeling about it in this chakra. So Archangel Uriel helps you to develop and trust your gut reactions.

He is the most glorious golden yellow and collects negativity to transmute it into light, just as your solar plexus does. The difference is that he does it on a vast scale and transmutes darkness into pure divine light.

Archangel Uriel's divine feminine counterpart is Archangel Aurora. Aurora means dawn and she too assists you to develop confidence and self worth especially when you are beginning a new project. Invoke her on your birthday, which is the start of a new year for you. Tell her what your hopes are for your year ahead and you may be amazed how she helps to bring about your greatest aspirations.

Archangel Aurora will help you develop something new and Archangel Uriel will give you the confidence and self worth to do it.

~ Archangels Jophiel and Christine ~

Archangel Jophiel is the angel of wisdom in charge of the crown chakra. This is known as the thousand petalled lotus because the head looks like a flower reaching up, while the spine is the stalk which takes the energy down to the earth. Each of the petals represents one of the qualities or aspects of God. When I was staying in Amma's ashram in Kerala one of the highlights of the day was the chanting of the thousand names of God, each of which represented one of the divine vibrations.

The crown chakra at the top of the head reaches up from the personality to the higher self and is fine tuned to receive the soul energy and filter it down into the lower chakras. Archangel Jophiel works with a yellow frequency to do this.

To help develop our divine wisdom and to connect more with our soul energy we can ask to go to Archangel Jophiel's retreat south of the Great Wall near Lanchow, North Central China in meditation or sleep. His name means 'Beauty of God'.

We were sent an Orb of one of Archangel Jophiel's angels radiating light over a residential street where there were several traffic humps or sleeping policemen. He was sending his energy into the road to give the drivers the wisdom to slow down as children played there. Angels are so very practical in the help they offer.

Archangel Christine, his twin flame, carries the feminine energy with the love, peace and protection of the Christ light. She will enfold you in wonderful light which uplifts and inspires you to greater aspirations.

~ Archangels Chamuel and Charity ~

Archangel Chamuel's name means 'He who sees God' and he is the archangel of love in charge of the heart chakra. He vibrates on the most delicate pink frequency of pure love and joy. Before I saw Orbs I knew mentally the colours of the archangels and had a sense of them but actually seeing them in photographs did more than confirm this knowing. It helped anchor their energy right into me. The pale pink light of Archangel Chamuel and his angels is gentle, compassionate, soft and heart warming. His retreat is at St Louis, Missouri, USA.

The first Orb I saw of Archangel Chamuel was sent to us by Kari Palmgren of Norway and I was bowled over. It had taken the shape of a beautiful pink heart with a pure white angel of love in the centre. We were told that when you look at it you receive love and joy and a desire to share it with others. You can see it in *Ascension Through Orbs*.

Paulette had never seen an angel and always wanted to. One day she invoked Archangel Chamuel to help her neighbour's dog which was pining for his mistress who had gone away. She sat quietly calling in the archangel of love over and over again. All at once she saw a beautiful pink light by the dog and knew it was Archangel Chamuel responding to her call. She also added that the dog perked up after that.

And the divine feminine counterpart to Archangel Chamuel is Archangel Charity, who is giving, generous and benevolent. She carries the deepest wisdom of the heart and shares it.

~ *Archangels Christiel and Mallory* ~

Archangel Christiel develops the causal chakra, the centre above the crown, which is the higher mind. He helps us to learn to silence this aspect of our mind, so that we can receive downloads of information from the spiritual realms and be at peace. This is the first of the transpersonal chakras, where we bring the light of our soul down into our mental body. Archangel Christiel is pure radiant white, with a mother of pearl sheen.

His twin flame, Archangel Mallory, is bringing in the divine feminine and is helping us to open our right brain, the creative, artistic, spiritual aspect of our mind. She is white magenta, the white of Christiel with a little of the magenta of the divine feminine.

~ *Archangels Zadkiel and Amethyst* ~

Archangel Zadkiel carries the violet light of transmutation. Where energy needs to be cleared and purified, his angels will come to help. His name means 'Righteousness of God'.

His light has prepared the way for the opportunities available in 2012. 2012 is mentioned, not just in the Mayan calendar, but in the legends of all ancient cultures as the end of the old times, the time of the lifting of the veil of illusion or our emergence from a cocoon into higher consciousness. This particular year marks the end of a 26,000 year astrological period, known as the outbreath of Brahma. During the following 20 year inbreath spiritual opportunities become available to enable more people to ascend than ever before.

The ancient, Wise Ones predicted that there would be a twenty five year period of purification to prepare the world for 2012. Accordingly, in 1987 at the Harmonic Convergence of that year, huge numbers of people rose early and went to sacred places to pray for help for the planet. St Germain, who has now been promoted to be the Lord of Civilization but was then the Master of the 7th ray, the violet ray, approached Source with the prayers. Archangel Zadkiel, under direction from Source, returned to St Germain the Violet Flame of Transmutation for the whole of humanity. Archangel Zadkiel and St Germain now work with the Violet Flame of Transmutation, which subsequently merged with the Silver Flame of Harmony and later the Gold Ray of Grace. It is now the mighty Gold and Silver Violet Flame of Grace, Harmony and Transmutation.

If we invoke this Flame, it can dissolve and transmute all lower vibrations within us on every level, from past lives to emotional, mental or physical blocks.

One of the most potent affirmations is I AM THE GOLD AND SILVER VIOLET FLAME. I AM refers to our monad or original divine spark which oversees our soul. When we affirm I AM it aligns us totally with that which we affirm. So in this case we are affirming that our divine essence is one with divine purity, harmony and grace. Grace really does enter and assist on many levels.

Because the gold and silver violet flame opens us up, as we repeat it, we need to place a psychic protection, such as Archangel Michael's cloak, round our auras first.

Modern digital cameras are at last able to give us many insights. Here are two stories told me about the Violet Flame. Susan is one of the angel teachers of the Diana Cooper School and she is also a heavy goods truck driver. She was driving a rather dangerous route where there had been a number of break-ins and her husband suggested that she apply for an alternative route. She replied that she was totally safe because she had put the silver violet flame round the truck. Later that day a picture was taken of her vehicle and you could clearly see the clouds of silver violet round it!

The second story was sent to me by Eileen Jarvis Langley, enclosing a photograph of a magnificent silver violet ray of light pouring down into her garden.

> *She said: Having spent quite a long time going round my garden invoking the Silver Violet Flame, I sat down and through my glasses I saw many small Orbs which I took to be reflections in my glasses, but on 'an impulse' I decided to go into the house to bring out my camera. The picture I enclose is a result of the second shot. Needless to say I was astounded, and I feel it is quite unmistakable as the Silver Violet Flame. This gave me so much confidence as I am studying the Angels through your Correspondence Course, and so thanked St. Germain and Archangel Zadkiel for my blessings.*

(You can see these photographs on www.dianacooper.com. They are quite amazing.)

Archangel Zadkiel's etheric retreat is in Cuba. His twin flame or divine feminine counterpart is an archangel known as Lady Amethyst. An amethyst crystal is the materialised form of her ray and carries the angelic light of transmutation and healing.

~ Archangels Mariel and Lavender ~

Archangel Mariel brings to us the wisdom of the divine feminine. He is in charge of the development of the higher aspect of the soul star chakra, the eleventh chakra, which is where we hold our ancestral links and pattern and he helps us to cleanse and clear this area of unhelpful links. He is a magnificent bright magenta.

His twin flame Lavender, is lavender in colour as her name suggests, and she brings in the softness of healing, purity and cleansing.

Like all the archangels, Mariel and Lavender collect energy from the sun to share with people as well as other angels.

~ Archangel Voku Monak ~

The Iranian Archangel Voku Monak revealed God's message to Zoroaster 2500 years ago. The Zoroastrians said that six archangels guarded the presence of Ahura Mazda, known as the Lord of Light or the Wise Lord. These archangels personified Good Wind, Excellent Truth,

THE ARCHANGELS AND UNIVERSAL ANGELS

Wished for Kingdom, Devotion, Wholesomeness and Non Death. It is said that Ahura Mazda flies in a disc of light and this is how he is depicted in ancient carvings.

~ Archangel Moroni ~

Archangel Moroni facilitated the discovery of divinely inscribed golden tablets which became the Book of Mormon, and established the Mormon religion.

~ Archangel Purlimiek ~

Archangel Purlimiek is the archangel in charge of the nature kingdom and the elementals. I have touched on the elemental kingdom in Chapter 25 on the Nature Kingdom. Archangel Purlimiek ensures that they are all working together in accordance with spiritual law for the highest good of the planet.

For example elves are earth elementals who work with trees. He designates angels to oversee groups of elves, to ensure that they are assisting the process of photosynthesis. The elves try to strengthen the spirit of a tree if it is invaded by bugs or ivy. In turn the angels in charge of the elves will inspire and encourage them. Trees are keepers of wisdom, who form a communication network across the world, and the elves help to hold their energy pure and clear. The energy needed for an oak tree is different from that needed to look after a beech or holly, so groups of elves see to individual species of trees. They can always refer to their angel, who in turn can call for help from Archangel Purlimiek.

Soil erosion in many parts of the world has become a problem. Archangel Purlimiek commands the nature angels who send troops of pixies to the different places to look after the structure of the soil. In some places sea water has soaked into the earth. The elementals cannot prevent this but they can help to restore the quality of the soil when the earth is reclaimed.

Pixies are also wonderful beings in their own right. Like all elementals, pixies respond very favourably to love and if you cherish your garden, they will work well with you, helping to ensure the quality of the soil is right. However they will not stay long for they are roving trouble shooters. They work with the bees to help pollinate flowers, so that nature can be abundant and Archangel Purlimiek guides and directs this operation.

In many parts of the world human activity, as well as negative human emotions, have diminished nature's bounty. However, the consciousness world wide is rising. People are beginning to honour the Earth again and there is a move towards local grown or even home grown food.

Tiny imps, who are only about 1" or 2.5 cms tall are made up of earth, air and water elements combined. They work with the pixies and their task is to aerate the soil. They also help seeds to grow. Where someone has green fingers you can be certain that they are listening to the imps.

Clearly the people of old who were in tune with nature and could see the elementals were aware how tiny and fun loving the imps were, which is why they called a mischievous child a wee imp.

Concrete and tarmac are stifling the earth so that Lady Gaia cannot breathe. Archangel Purlimiek's angels keep whispering to town planners and individuals alike to set the earth free. However, many humans are no longer listening to the quiet, still angelic voices who are communicating with them. Where the ground is covered in bricks and mortar, tarmac and concrete, eventually nature unleashes its power and something erupts. It may be as a flood, fire, volcano, earthquake or in some other way but there is always a reaction.

I rejoiced the other day when I saw a small but determined flower which had managed to force its way through a tarmac road and was holding its tiny petals up to the sun. It was a reminder of the power of nature.

Archangel Purlimiek also works with those wonderful elementals, the dragons, who can be of air, earth or fire, or a combination of all three elements. They offer enormous wisdom, courage, love, strength, protection and companionship to humans. If they bond with you, the link will never break and they become your friend and protector for life. They love fun and are especially good at befriending sensitive, high frequency children and will protect their spirits when they travel in the inner planes at night.

In recent years as Earth is moving towards ascension Archangel Purlimiek has invited new elementals here to help with the cleansing of the planet. They come from another universe and are delighted to have the opportunity to serve Lady Gaia and also to learn about our world. Esaks are air elementals who help to hoover up negativity above the ground. For example if a party has been held where drugs and alcohol are abused or people are polluting a place with anger, they will arrive to clear up the psychic mess.

John and Mary, a newly married couple, sent us a picture of their home after a flood. Everything looked dismal. However, beavering away to clear the mess were tiny little esaks consuming the psychic debris and trying their best to help.

Kyhils are water elementals who are helping to transmute the negativity in the waters of the world, a huge and much needed task.

Not only is Archangel Purlimiek in overall charge of the natural world of Earth but he works with Archangel Butyalil, the cosmic angel in charge of the stars and energies round the planet. He also liaises with Archangel Gersisa, the great angel of inner Earth who looks after the ley lines and movements within the earth. In addition he aligns with Archangel Fhelyai, who is in charge of the animal kingdom. Naturally he communicates with all the other archangels as well.

When you see a beautiful sunset, a majestic tree, the eternal sea or a mountain remember to thank Archangel Purlimiek

~ *Archangel Fhelyai* ~

Archangel Fhelyai is in charge of the welfare of animals, both on Earth and when they pass over. His name is pronounced Felyay and the angels wanted us to know this because when we sound a name, the vibration is important. It calls in a person, animal or angel.

If an animal is sick we can ask Archangel Fhelyai to heal, support and encourage it. If it is ready to pass, its loved ones in spirit will arrive to help. In the case of a much loved domestic pet or occasional farm animal the spirits of its human as well as animal friends, will be there to assist it. If the animal is a wild one the animal spirits of those who have loved it will be close. It is easy to imagine a family animal like an elephant being surrounded by its ancestors on passing. But the same applies to all animals. They all had a mother or brothers and sisters.

Just like humans, animals incarnate into a physical body to experience life on Earth. They too are learning about love. Archangel Fhelyai works with all the archangels and angels to support the animal kingdom.

A friend of mine, Sue Stone, author of *Love Life Live Life*, is an animal lover. The family keep several horses and they love their chickens, who range freely in their large garden. Her twin sons look after the hens and are very protective of them. One day she phoned to tell me this story.

*Her sons were going out so they popped their heads round her
door to remind her to shut the chickens in the coop because
they were all outside and it was late afternoon. She promised
to do so but then the phone rang.*

*The inevitable happened as she chatted away to her friend.
She forgot about them. She was looking idly out of the window
as she exchanged news with her friend when to her horror she
saw a large brown fox heading along the hedge towards the
hen house. Dropping the phone she ran outside, calling on the
angels to protect them. When she reached the chicken run,
to her relief and amazement, every single one was inside the
coop and the door was firmly shut.*

For one of our Orbs books Kathy Crosswell and I were sent a picture of
a little dog with the golden Orb of Archangel Fhelyai very close to her.
We were told that she passed over a few days later and we know that she
had received all the assistance she needed.

When a human passes, they are taken to the other side by angels where
they are greeted by friends and family. Then they receive spiritual healing, assessment and education or whatever else they need for the prog-
ress of their soul. In the inner planes some undertake tasks with which
they are already familiar from their experiences on Earth. Others train
to do something new. A few move into universal work or return to their
planets of origin. However, work is not onerous; rather it is a joyous
expression of personal talents and creativity. A percentage of humans
decide to reincarnate quickly to repay karma, which is a method of
learning, while more evolved souls may return to Earth to teach or help
the world in some way.

In current times an increasing number of people are ascending when
they pass over, in which case they are met by archangels and ascended
masters and conducted ceremoniously and joyously into the heavens.

Animals are not inferior to humans, just different. Some are less
evolved and others more so. When they die their experience is similar
to that of humans. Once they leave their physical bodies they are free
spirits, who are taken by one of Archangel Fhelyai's angels to meet their
loved ones on the other side. Then they receive healing, assessment or
education. They too delight in their freedom and opportunity for joyous expression. Then their souls may choose to reincarnate, return to
their home planet or stay for a while in the inner planes.

People have so often told me of their dreams where they meet their beloved animals in the spiritual worlds and are delighted to find them happy and free and full of love.

Betty's dog was very old and full of arthritis when he died. He had been really stiff and in a lot of pain for some years and for some time she was torn about whether he should be put down or not. The vet said to her, 'You will know when the time is right.' And indeed she did. One day she just knew she had to say goodbye to him but it was a heartbreaking decision.

A few weeks later she had a very vivid dream in which she met him. He bounded up to her full of life force and vitality like a puppy. He told her that he was grateful for the extra years as he had learnt a lot but that she made the right decision at the end, for he knew it was done from love. And now he was so pleased to be free.

She felt overwhelming love flowing between them and then she woke up. She cried when she told me about her experience but they were tears of pure love and joy.

If you need guidance about an animal ask Archangel Fhelyai to help you.

~ Universal Angels Roquiel and Joules ~

Roquiel works deep in the Earth, taking the connection of the Earth Star deeper into Lady Gaia. His colour is black and he takes in all the energy that comes down through the chakras of those who are ready to open up to the highest. He holds it and gives it to Gaia or directs it to the leylines and portals.

He helps the Stellar Gateway and the Earth Star chakras to open simultaneously. His retreat is in Uluru, Australia.

Joules is the twin flame of Archangel Roquiel; the feminine energy. She works deep in the oceans and one of her tasks is to govern the alignment of the tectonic plates. Her retreat is deep in the ocean in the middle of the Bermuda Triangle.

~ Archangels Butyalil and Gersisa ~

Archangel Butyalil is a universal angel who keeps in order the vast currents of the universe that impact on Earth. He carries masculine energy and is pure white.

When he enters the orbit of our planet he steps his energy down through the Pyramids. Interestingly his retreat is above Earth in the central point where the four stars Neptune, Pleiades, Orion and Sirius meet. They are known as the ascension stars because they have a vital role in the ascension of Earth.

Archangel Butyalil's role is so vast that he communicates and works in co-operation with the archangels of other planets and also Archangel Purlimiek of the Nature Kingdom. The unicorns are actively assisting him, as is Archangel Metatron and the Seraphim Seraphina.

Naturally he also works with his twin flame Archangel Gersisa, who carries the feminine energy. Just as Archangel Butyalil connects with the cosmic beings above the Earth, Archangel Gersisa is in alignment with those who work within the Earth Kingdom. Her retreat is in Hollow Earth, right in the core of the planet.

One of her roles is to assist Archangels Sandalphon and Roquiel to clear the Earth Star chakras of humanity, so that divine light can come right down into the planet. She also looks after the leylines and helps to keep them cleansed, working with the energy of the full moon to strength and align the planetary grid. Archangel Gersisa's energy is grey, a merging of black and white.

~ Archangel Azrael ~

Archangel Azrael is an archangel in the Hebrew and Muslim traditions. His name means, 'whom God helps'.

He is known as the Archangel of Spirit because he is an intermediary between angels, archangels and anything spiritual. He is the only angel not to have an aura because his light is within him, so that he is translucent but does not radiate out. He often wears a black cloak and has black wings because he is quiet and still, offering comfort where it is needed, especially at times of bereavement. He is with you when you die, soothing any suffering, and helps with the journey as you pass over.

If someone is at peace when they are dying, they surrender to Archangel Azrael, slipping into his arms and allow themselves to be taken away. He reminds them that death is transformation.

When many people are passing at the same time, for example when there has been a major disaster, Archangel Azrael will travel to the scene with many other archangels in order to help those who have just died. They also bring the spirits of loved ones from the other side, so that they can encourage and assist their friends and relatives to cross over.

He stands in the background at a birth, while Archangel Gabriel radiates light as he connects the new spirit with the physical body of the baby.

Archangel Azrael also works with Archangel Metatron, helping to keep the Akashic records.

CHAPTER 27

The Orders Of Angels

It is widely believed that angels were created by Source before humans were added to the universal scheme of things. When humans were created some of the angels who vibrated on a slower frequency, more in tune with ours, were delegated to look after us.

Angels radiate at different frequencies, with various tasks assigned to each one. Imagine a shop full of coloured silks, each with its own vibration. These are woven into a harmonious tapestry, where each colour is perfect and important. No colour is better than another for each has a task and complements those around it. This is like the angelic realm where every angel is considered equal but different.

Those who have the fastest frequencies are the Seraphim, Cherubim and Thrones.

On a slower frequency band are the Dominions, Virtues and Powers.

The third band are the Principalities, archangels and angels, who vibrate more slowly.

Interestingly many archangels span the dimensions. We may connect with them at the archangel frequency but some expand across every energy band.

~ Seraphim ~

The fastest frequency of angel is the Seraphim, whose essence is pure love. They are the heavenly hosts who constantly sing the praises of the Creator and sound the harmonics which hold the vibration of Creation. This maintains creation and they direct the divine energy as it emanates from Source. They are attuned to accept a high level of God-force.

The Seraphim each have different tasks and vibrate at a variety of frequencies but they are all of equal stature.

They do not usually work with humans but they do add energy to projects of importance to humanity and they do communicate with us from time to time.

~ Cherubim ~

The Cherubim, the angels of wisdom, are guardians of the stars and the celestial heavens. They help you feel a sense of the wonder and sheer awesomeness of the universes. They also help you to connect unconsciously to your planet of origin, to give you a sense of peace. If you wish to work with the Cherubim you really need to purify yourself and raise your vibration. The unicorns can help you with this if you invoke them.

~ Cherubs ~

Cherubs work with the Cherubim and help with the stars. They work with people who are angel ambassadors.

During the Renaissance many mystics and people whose third eyes were opened by fever, saw cherubs, which is why artists depicted them so often. In fact they were seeing a tiny energy fragment of Cherubim, who resonated at too high a frequency to be visible to humans.

Cherubs were seen as babies because they emanated joy and pure childlike innocence. People who felt vulnerable connected with them. So too did those who love the stars and the cosmos.

~ Thrones ~

The Thrones look after and guard the planets. The angel in charge of our planet, Earth, is therefore a Throne.

Ezekiel, the Hebrew prophet describes them as flaming torches or burning coals of fire. They are often depicted as having many eyes, or even wheels.

This trio, the Seraphim, Cherubim and Thrones, receive direct illumination from Source and they transform the light in order to transmit it at a level that can be accepted by slower frequencies in the universe.

~ Dominions ~

The Dominions are celestial prefects, who look after those angels whose tasks require them to vibrate at a slower frequency. They are channels of mercy and although they rarely connect with humans they help to smooth the passage between the spiritual and the material.

~ Virtues ~

The Virtues send out vast beams of light in a form accessible to us humans. These are the angels who make miracles happen. When groups raise their consciousness and tune into angel energy, they access the pool of information the Virtues radiate. They facilitate the rise in consciousness for the New Age.

~ Powers ~

We may never have heard of the Powers but most of us have heard of the angels of birth and death. The angel of birth, who lovingly enfolds us at our moment of birth, is a Power as is the angel who joyously helps us with our transition from our human body into the light body at death. These angels help and guide us to the light at our passing. The Lords of Karma, who are in overall charge of the karmic records, are Powers. They guard the conscience of humankind. There are also Lords of Group Karma, National Karma, World Karma and Universal Karma.

~ Principalities ~

Principalities look after and protect cities, nations, multinational corporations and any very large configuration of people. Like all the angelic hosts they work throughout the universe, and Earth is a very small part of their domain. When we have problems with our community affairs, we can address the Principalities for assistance.

~ Archangels ~

The archangels are in charge of big projects and also look after the angels. See the chapter on individual archangels (26).

~ Angels ~

There are many kinds of angels, who undertake different tasks. Guardian angels are particularly selected because their slower frequency matches that of humans. While they guard us from birth, they are also available to guide and help us in many ways, if only we will ask. They can smooth our path, heal through us, inspire us and work with us to create a harmonious life and spread the light.

Angels are our guardians on Earth. We each have a personal guardian angel, who is a recording angel. In other words our guardian angel notes our thoughts and deeds and keeps our individual akashic records up to date. These are overseen by Lords of Karma.

CHAPTER 28

Angels From The Bible

Angels appear throughout the Christian Bible, serving a variety of functions.

~ Messenger Angels ~

The best known of these are the messengers who appeared at the time of the birth of Jesus, the Christ. Before Mary's wedding to Joseph, an angel appeared to Mary and told her that she would bear a son, who would be the son of God.

It seems that Joseph was not receptive to angels when he was fully awake, so one came to him in a dream to inform him that indeed Mary's child would be the Messiah. Then an angel appeared to shepherds to tell them that their saviour had been born and they were surrounded by a whole host of angels singing, "Glory be to God in heaven and on Earth be peace."

The wise men followed a shining star to the stable where Jesus was born. They had been asked by Herod to tell him where the child was but angels warned them not to go back to Herod and they left the country by a different route. When Herod in a rage ordered the death of every boy under the age of two, again an angel warned Joseph in a dream, so that he and Mary fled with their son to Egypt.

On another occasion two shining white angels appeared to the disciples to give them the message that Jesus had been taken from Earth to Heaven — and in the same way He would return from Heaven to Earth.

People were receptive to angels in the early Christian times just as they are becoming again. Cornelius was a Roman centurion in Caesarea. He was a good man, married to a Jewish wife. One day he heard an angel call his name and tell him to go to Simon's house, where Peter lodged.

In the meantime Peter was praying on a rooftop when he was shown a vision. He saw an enormous sheet tied at the corners and filled with all kinds of animals including pigs, goats, lambs, wolves and chickens. A voice told him to choose and eat.

Peter was a Jew and unable to eat meat not killed according to Jewish law. He said so. The angelic voice replied, "What God calls fit, let no mortal call unfit." He saw the vision twice more and heard the same words. As he left the roof, Roman soldiers were hammering on the door. The angel told him to go with them and fear nothing for they had been sent by Jesus.

The soldiers took him to Cornelius who implored him to teach and baptise all the people he had gathered. Many of the elders were horrified. They thought that non-Jews should not become Christians. Peter, however, remembered what the angel said, "What God calls fit, let no mortal think unfit."

He reminded the elders that God accepts everyone. A rushing wind was heard, which was presumably the sound of angels' wings, and tongues of fire flickered above the crowd.

~ Rescuing Angels ~

Angels do save humans from danger. Daniel was placed in a den of hungry lions where he would starve to death even if the lions did not kill him. However, an angel was sent to a farmer called Habbakuk, who had just packed a basket of food. The angel carried him with the basket to the lions' den where the terrified farmer gave the food to Daniel.

Presumably the angel did not need to save Daniel from the lions or else he would have done so. In ancient times initiates were trained in the temples to hold their thoughts totally steady, without fear, so that they could control lions, snakes or any other creature. In some lifetime Daniel must have had this training.

When Nebuchadnezzar was king in Babylon three Jews called Shadrach, Meshach and Abednego refused to worship the huge statue he had built. They were told that they would be chained and thrown into the fiery furnace if they did not worship the idol.

When they still refused, they were indeed thrown into the fiery furnace. Instead of the usual screams when people burnt to death, the watching dignitaries heard only singing. A white-faced Nebuchadnezzar pointed at the flames and said he could see the three men and an angel walking in the flames and singing.

The king ordered them out and they stepped from the flames. The fire had melted the chains which had fallen away. Their bodies, hair and clothes were untouched and instead of the smell of singed flesh, only the perfume of flowers could be smelt.

~ Angels of Destruction ~

There are also angels of destruction. The old and bad is destroyed to make way for the new and good. This is also the task of Shiva, the Hindu God (or angel).

There was a city called Sodom in which all sorts of lust and licentiousness were practised. Abraham pleaded with God not to destroy the honest and good people as well as the debauched ones. God promised that if ten honest people could be found, all the people of the city would be spared. However, only one honest person, a man called Lot, could be discovered living in Sodom and God's angels destroyed the city.

Now it may well be that a physical earthquake caused the destruction of the area but the angels oversee all of nature, including earthquakes.

CHAPTER 29

Angels In Churches

Most of us have gone into a church or cathedral sometime and felt a sense of peace and stillness. This is because angels have contained the energy in that sacred space for centuries.

The angel of a church can also be extremely protective. A friend of mine decided to have a very quiet, meditative Christmas. She went to a church to sit alone. As she entered she felt the presence of a golden angel filling the church. She told me she had a sense of how strong, how powerful and how fierce it was. This was not a frightening experience. Rather it was reassuring to know that the angel was so immense and so protective. She felt safe and enfolded within its energy. It is the only experience of this kind she has ever had.

People very often have spiritual and angelic experiences when they are out in nature. This is because the angels do not judge or criticise us. Surrounded only by the angels of trees, rocks, mountains and streams, who accept us as we are, we are safe. When we feel this security we can relax our guard. This is when we open up to the spiritual dimensions.

In a church, or to be more accurate, in a building used for spiritual purposes, there can be a similar feeling of safety. If the congregations are spiritual enough to be non-judgemental and accepting of all, then the place is steeped in the peace that allows us to still our minds and open our hearts.

There is much noise, disharmony, excitement and violence in the world. We can never find the path to Source when we are constantly busy and distracted. Churches and temples are usually quiet, peaceful places where we can centre ourselves.

In order to connect to our intuition we must become still. To find our wisdom we must listen in silence. When we sit daily in inner peace and quiet our way forward is revealed and smoothed. It is when we connect to Source that we find true refreshment for our spirit. It is in the stillness of our hearts and minds that our emptiness can be filled with love.

When we become calm and centred we radiate such wonderful waves of peace around us that people want to bathe in our sea of harmony.

The angels of nature, of churches and of truly spiritual places help to calm and soothe troubled minds and hearts. They provide a quiet, safe place where this connection can be made.

Jeanne, whose story I told in Chapter 8, went to the Domo in Florence. She stood in a group of people at the back of the Domo and relaxed in the energy. She felt nothing on the left of the cathedral. Then she had a terrific feeling inside her and her eyes were drawn to a space on the right. There was such an enormous loving presence emanating from the right that she found herself riveted. It reached all the way up to the ceiling and filled the space. Despite her frustration that she could not see this huge angel, she could feel the loving presence so strongly that her heart felt as if it was being opened and expanded.

When you relax into

the love of angels,

your heart

will be opened.

CHAPTER 30

Dark Angels

We have been fed with stories of dark angels or fallen angels who have rebelled against God and become evil and vengeful. They are known as Lucifer, Satan, Mephistopheles, Samael or Beelzebub amongst other names. All religions refer to dark angels or gods who tempt or destroy. I believe it is only on planet Earth, the plane of free choice and duality, that these dark forces could gain credence.

In Isaiah God says, "I form the Light and create Darkness." The Creator was always considered to be the source of creation and destruction. It was only two hundred years before the birth of Christ that a belief evolved in a separate force for evil which opposed God.

Source is omnipotent, is light.
God is not in competition with evil or the devil,
rather He allows them to serve His purpose.

The popular legend is that Lucifer, a Seraph, Bearer of the Light, and beloved of God, challenged Him for his throne. God cast the rebel into the abyss and one-third of the angel host defected from the light with him, becoming dark angels who tempt people into evil, lustful ways.

Ultimately all angels serve Source. It is not possible for archangels to defect. Angels and archangels do not rebel against the Creator. What they do is offer their services to God, in this case to test and challenge those on planet Earth.

Earth is unique in that Source decided to set up a free will experiment here. What greater way for beings to grow and experience than to have choice?

The reason for the experiment was this. A state of perfection is not a state of growth. In order to expand, there must be a challenge. There is no yin without yang, no negative without positive, no feminine without masculine. So Earth was designated as a plane of choice where beings could learn to balance the material and spiritual. By experiencing both polarities the consciousness of the beings incarnating here would expand and would enrich Source when we return Home.

When Source set up this free will zone, nothing less than a great archangel was needed to oversee the divine project. I believe Archangel Lucifer volunteered to lead this experiment in free choice. We are repeatedly told that Lucifer will one day be reinstated to his original place. This will be when all on planet Earth raise their consciousness and integrate their shadow side. Then his task will be done.

In order to participate in the free will experiment, Lucifer and his volunteers also agreed to be shut off from their connection with Source. Once in the dark Lucifer swung to the negative pole and used his enormous power for evil and temptation.

The Creator decreed that all who incarnate here are free to choose their thoughts and actions. Although the spark of divinity remains within us, the memory of our divine heritage was closed down. So on Earth we have total liberty to think negative or positive thoughts, do bad or good deeds. Our growth depends on our personal choice. Furthermore whatever we think, do or believe is mirrored back to us in our lives. This means that each one of us creates our individual reality. When we change our beliefs, thoughts or acts, the universal energy reflects the changes back to us, so we have a different life.

In other words, on Earth our inner world is reflected by the outer world. This gives us maximum chances for spiritual growth. We grow by facing the tests presented. Every time we make a choice of right thinking or right deeds, we grow lighter. In planes where there is no free choice, growth is slower.

Darkness, negativity or evil is absence of light or lack of spiritual knowledge. When we are in the dark, we feel separate from Source. It hurts and it is only a hurt being who will harm another.

Disconnection from the light lets in guilt, fear and self-deception. When we forget Source or believe we are alone and separate, we depend on and hold onto people. This means we falsely try to please people or control them to avoid the feeling of aloneness. And so the darkness within us grows.

The forgetting of spiritual truths meant that people made choices to hurt others, to destroy the planet, to focus on material possessions and think dark, angry thoughts. The dark angels fed on this negativity and grew in power.

It is very difficult not to be tainted by negativity while we are in a physical body. Even the most beautiful spirits find it hard to withstand the darkness of our planet. Despite the risk of our light being engulfed by the blanket of darkness in this plane, souls from all over the universe wait to incarnate on planet Earth because of the unique challenges and opportunities it offers.

Those who become very negative or closed to the truth will often continue on that path until they feel so hurting that they cry out for help. The angels of light respond to these cries and help them start on their journey back to Source.

Just as angels of light use their power to help, encourage and free people, the dark angels strive to tempt, to whisper thoughts of anger or destruction and to weaken humans. In the free will zone of planet Earth, the dark angels will do anything to achieve their ends, even impersonate light angels. The greatest protections against the voices of darkness, or temptation, are common sense and discrimination as well as good intention and positivity — and always listening to the still quiet voice of conscience within.

If an angel or any other being appears to us, it is always appropriate to challenge whether they are truly of the light. Suitable wording might be, "In the name of God and all that is holy, are you an angel of light?" Challenge in the same words three times. If the answer is "Yes" each time, then accept them. Under the great Spiritual Laws of the universe, they must speak truthfully if challenged three times in the name of God.

True angels have a golden quality and radiance. This quality is reflected in their whispers into your mind. If the whispers are of love and harmony, justice and acceptance, then they come from the light angels. A light angel will always leave us feeling warm and peaceful.

Angels of light say, "Follow your heart. This is your higher purpose."

Do light angels have free will? The answer is no. Angels' greatest desire is to serve God — to do the will of the Creator. This limits choice. When we humans too rise in consciousness so that our only desire is to follow the will of Source, we will no longer want the freedom to destroy ourselves or others.

We must always remember that the Divine Intelligence is overseeing the project and light is always more powerful than darkness. No dark force can touch us if we hold onto the light.

During the experiment of free will, humans have overstepped the bounds of what is allowed. We have damaged each other and the planet. This is why there is such a massive rescue mission taking place by angels and other light forces to help us. It is imperative we relax, trust, centre and calm ourselves, so that they can get closer.

Like humans dark angels who have separated themselves from Source for this experiment have freedom to do as they will.

Light angels have no free will

for their only desire is to

serve the will of the Creator.

CHAPTER 31

Rescuing Angels

It is during times of danger that people turn to spirit. It takes life-threatening situations for many to remember that there is help available. Perhaps this is why many modern representations of angels are found in military establishments! For instance I understand that there is a beautiful stained glass window at a naval base in California showing Archangel Gabriel.

The appearance of angels at Mons during the First World War has been well reported. It seems that when the British were being defeated by the Germans, angels appeared above the armies and were seen by hundreds of soldiers. According to reports some saw one angel, others a whole host of them. However, it is agreed that the angels intervened to encourage the British army and give it time to disengage.

I am sure that the angels responded to millions of prayers being sent out for both sides by those in the army and those at home. Inevitably the beings of light supported freedom versus aggression and control.

During the Battle of Britain there were aircraft in which the crews had been killed, which continued to fight. Air Chief Marshal Lord Dowding believed that these aircraft were piloted by angels.

As I was writing this a friend told me that her father had had an angel experience when he was a teenager. He had never mentioned it to her but he had told her mother, who years later had told her.

It happened when he was eighteen and on his first motorbike. The bike skidded in the rain and he was thrown off. By the time the ambulance arrived he was semiconscious. Then as they were about to put him into the ambulance, he heard the soft fluttery sound of wings and felt a wonderful warm safe presence gently lifting him with the ambulance men. He knew it was an angel and that he would be all right.

I wonder if and how it changed his life? Or did he like so many others put the experience into a corner of his mind and shut the door?

Before we come into incarnation, we discuss our life purpose with the Lords of Karma, those in the angel realms who oversee our balance sheets of accountability. We choose our time of birth according to the availability of appropriate parents for the experience we need. We decide on the planetary aspects that will affect us. More evolved souls are very careful about the conditions for their incarnation and therefore fewer choices are available to them.

We predetermine the length of our life and the time of our departure. The latter decision can be varied by certain choices during our lifetime. If, for instance, we allow our physical body to fall into disrepair by bad diet, it may no longer be able comfortably to house our spirit. If we lose the will to live or commit suicide, we may die before our time but no one can do so without the permission of their Higher Self and God. There are many forms of suicide. People drink themselves to death. They take ridiculous risks against their intuition. They die of a broken heart. They send out such powerfully negative thoughts that they become ill. Our angels are trying to assist us, however wilful we are.

If we abort our mission on Earth, we have to re-do it with similar circumstances and challenges. If we leave ten years early for instance before we complete one last karmic repayment, we may only need to come back to this planet for ten years to repay the debt. In that case we will die in our next life as a child. The angels will support us whatever we choose.

However, if it is definitely not our time to die, then our angel will save us. They may even do this in a physical way. There are many reports of people feeling a rush of warm air and finding themselves being pushed by an unseen force out of danger.

There was a wartime expression that if a bullet had your number on it your time was up. If it was not your time you were safe. The angels were protecting you. More and more people are reporting near-death experiences. Throughout cultures and religions these stories are remarkably consistent. The most commonly reported is that in which someone is moving along a tunnel of light with a wonderful sense of peace and love but an angel, a being of light or a voice tells them their task is not finished and they must return to complete it.

In other cases an angel or shining wise person, who is presumably a representative of the Lords of Karma, takes them to review their situation and offers them a choice to return and change their lives.

There are no accidental deaths for our angels will

rescue us if it is not our time to leave the planet.

CHAPTER 32

Angel Wisdom

Angels serve spirit. True spirituality is beyond religion, though it accepts and honours all of them. At the top of the mountain all is One but the lower down the mountain we are, the further we have moved from the pure message of spirit and the more dissent there is between religions.

True spirituality looks at that mountain and sees that every path up to Source is right for the person climbing it — even pain and disease, even hurt and disaster are pathways. The pain, the disease, the hurt, the disaster are often the challenges which turn people to spirit. The deepest despair is often the pit from which people call out to spirit for help.

Those who unconsciously work for the darkness, sadly often in the name of God and religion, seek to control, constrict or disempower others. They may say, "You will only reach the mountain top if you do it this way". They may even refuse to help someone out of a situation unless the person follows their path. This demonstrates control and manipulation, narrow mindedness and lack of compassion. If anyone tries to restrict or imprison another in the name of the light, they do a terrible disservice to the planet and inevitably bear awful karma for it.

> *God-fearing people walk in the dark.*
> *God-loving people grow towards the light.*
> *Angel-fearing people live in the shadow.*
> *Angel-loving people dance with joy.*

To promote ignorance keeps the light from people. Those who knowingly conceal the truth or distort it on the pretext that the masses are not ready to hear it, serve the darkness. Throughout history, sacred and esoteric texts have been hidden away or destroyed.

In AD 553 at the Second Council of Constantinople, the Emperor Justinian had reincarnation written out of the Bible. He and the church wanted to claim power over people's souls.

When this truth is revealed and the sacred Laws of Reincarnation are recognised each one of us will know that our every action is recorded by our guardian angel in the akashic records and that we ourselves can take charge of our destiny. No one will give authority to intermediaries in the religious hierarchies to tell them what they may or may not do on their path to the light.

Do not feel angry and frustrated as you read this. Instead calmly ask the angels to help bring the truth to light. Ask them to open the minds of those in charge of controlling the masses on the planet. Ask them to light up the religious and world leaders.

Religions tell people what to do and what to believe. Spirituality tells people to listen for their own guidance and follow their hearts. It leaves people free, reminding us only of the highest qualities like harmlessness, love, joy, compassion, integrity, brotherhood, sisterhood, peace and oneness. Even saying these words ignites a light within us.

Anyone who preaches hellfire and damnation is energising the darkness and therefore working for it. These preachers add to the fear in our universe. Every single time we say with fear the names which personalise the devil, the vibration of the name increases his power. Even swearing has a vibration which lowers our potential.

At the beginning of the fifteenth century, the priesthood was tainted with corruption. When this happened the priests stopped defending the angels, the light. Instead they resisted and attacked the devil,thus energizing the dark and allowing the horrors of the Inquisition to take place. However when they killed the witches, they were in reality eliminating the healers, the seers, prophets and those of the truth. Many of these souls are now reincarnating to bring the light back to Earth.

A truly spiritual person will trust people to find their own way to the top of the mountain and will assist impartially. If someone wants to move to a different path, an enlightened being will wish them well and will not judge someone who takes a wrong turn. He or she will encourage others to think for themselves, to listen to their inner guidance and be independent. They will empower everyone to speak directly to Source or angels or beings of great wisdom.

Angels of light will help anyone climbing any path up that mountain. All are equal. And even if some are slithering downwards, angels will patiently stand by without judgement to help when they are asked.

People sometimes ask how it is that angels speak so many different languages. Most of us are telepathic. We often pick up what other people are thinking and usually we say in surprise, "Oh, I was just thinking that!" Beyond the limitations of the body, in the spiritual realms, all communication is telepathic. Words are not needed because the energy of what is being communicated is transferred to the other person. This is not done haphazardly and unconsciously in the way we tend to do it.

When angelic beings communicate with us they direct a stream of consciousness to us which reaches us as a powerful thought or voice in our head. Sound may be added to create a voice. However, it is the energy which is transferred and then filtered through our consciousness in our language. So angels do not need to be linguists. They communicate in the language of the Creator, the vibration of love.

At the first angel workshop I ran, I was guiding a meditation. I was clearly told that we were all being too analytical and must stop thinking. Instead we must fill our minds with the colour white-violet. Immediately I felt an immense white-violet light flame in my third eye. I had the most incredible sensation of peace and oneness. Afterwards I discovered that many had felt this same powerful feeling as the angels came closer. To immerse ourselves in the colour white-violet or violet will increase our vibratory rate.

So there are five ways to connect more closely with angels of light.

1. Think about them frequently. Ask them to come closer and help.
2. Cleanse and purify your thoughts so that your auric field is more penetrable to their fine vibration.
3. Stop analysing and overthinking everything. This puts you in your left brain and prevents the connection. Whenever you find yourself in your head, place a white-violet light in your mind.
4. Be receptive to their presence and their messages.
5. Listen to angel music. This is now being channelled by a number of sources. It refines your vibrations allowing angels to penetrate your aura. It is truly beautiful. How do you know if it is genuine? How do you know if it is right for you? Use your intuition.

Angels help you

claim authority

over your own soul.

CHAPTER 33

Inspiration

One day I was sitting quietly thinking about the many problems that people I knew were facing. Suddenly an angelic voice impressed itself. It said, "The reason so many of you are going through challenges is because karma is speeding up. You must face your demons, learn your lessons and move on. There is no time for rests now."

Karma is the inevitable repayment of our debts. If we have ever thought or done something to hurt or harm another, we have to repay. There is no escaping the consequence of our actions for the balance sheet of karma is kept over all our lifetimes.

I had been going through a period of difficulty myself. Even though I was trying to keep centred and steady through this challenge, I knew that my emotions were fluctuating.

"How can we help and heal others when we feel like this?" I questioned.

The angelic voice replied, "Get out of your personality into your golden body. It is your angelic body."

I smiled when it said that. The golden body is an expression I use to mean a state of centred detachment. The expression originated some years ago when I was working with a clairvoyant client who looked at me and said with a gasp, "Oh, you are completely golden. You're in your golden body."

When we shift gear into our golden body we are in a space in which nothing and no one outside us can affect us. We leave our personality behind so we are listening to higher guidance and are totally focused on what we are doing.

The voice continued with what was totally astonishing information to me, "Because this is an especially difficult time now, angels are moving close to planet Earth to help. Your atoms, cells and DNA are being changed, so that you can enter the fifth dimension. You may feel the sensations in your body — in your heart, shoulders, solar plexus and new budding chakras."

Most human beings have been living in a physical world where we believe in the existence of only that which we can see, feel and touch. We have been living in a material world, limited by our beliefs.

We constantly need love and approval from others. We fear rejection, abandonment and aloneness. This means that we humans try to control and manipulate others to get these needs met. Needing physical, mental and emotional support leads to co-dependent relationships. Such relationships stunt our spiritual growth. When we do turn to spirit, most of us ask for things we want or think we need.

Planet Earth is to become a fifth-dimensional planet, which is a planet of higher consciousness. In this state of consciousness we do not need support or approval from other humans, so we no longer seek co-dependent relationships. Our sole aim is to follow our highest spiritual purpose.

At these spiritual dimensions we are living at a greater level of trust, so when we ask for something from God or Source we expect to receive. In any case we are focused on asking for the development of qualities rather than things.

In the fifth dimension we will live in a state of harmony, peace and detachment, working for the highest good of ourselves and all others. Now our challenges are initiations to come closer to Source.

No wonder angels with all their love and wisdom are flocking near to planet Earth to help in this massive shift in consciousness!

The voice continued, "You can connect with angels more easily when you are in a fifth-dimensional body, which is your golden body. Moving into this spiritual state of consciousness is like shifting gear. Most of you do it automatically but there are things that help.

–   Read inspirational books. This will keep you open to spirit.
–   Focus on beauty, joy and beautiful qualities.
–   Walk in and enjoy nature as often as you can.
–   Listen to inspirational music. Music enters your cells and lifts your vibratory levels.
–   Constantly say thank you for the things that you do have. When you say thank you, you send out an energy of appreciation which attracts more good things into your life.
–   Relax. We know this is difficult when you feel you are hurtling along in the river of life but we ask you to trust and let the flow take you.

I asked how to connect with angels. The voice replied, "Simply focus on angels!"

To bring angels into your life,

focus on angels.

CHAPTER 34

Angel Exercises

I end this book with some guided journeys to help you to become closer to your angels and allow them to help you in ways which you may never have thought possible.

Make sure that you are wearing comfortable clothing and will not be disturbed for half an hour.

To raise the energy in the room you may care to light a candle and have crystals, plants or flowers around you. Spiritual books in the room also help to lift the vibrations in order to connect with angels, as does beautiful music.

Before you start your inner work, put out the intention that whatever happens is for your highest good. Ask for the angels of light to come to you to protect and heal you.

EXERCISE: *To meet your angel*

1. Sit or lie comfortably.
2. Breathe slightly more deeply than usual, relaxing on the outbreath until your whole body feels calm.
3. Invite your guardian angel to come close. Feel its gentle wings enfold you and relax into the safety.
4. Ask your guardian angel its name. Rejoice if its name comes into your mind but don't worry if it doesn't.
5. Enfolded in the love and security of your guardian angel, become aware of other angels around you and how much love each has for you.
6. Breathe in all the love available to you. Remind yourself you deserve to be loved.
7. When you are ready open your eyes gently.

EXERCISE: *To cleanse and heal your heart*

1. Sit or lie comfortably.
2. Take a deep breath and, as you let it out, centre yourself. Then on each outbreath, say 'calm' to yourself, until you feel really relaxed.
3. Sense the outside of your heart. Is it smooth and healthy or is it rough, bruised, cracked, broken or hurt in any way?
4. Sense inside your heart. Is it full of love or is it full of hurt, anger or jealousy? Are there old unresolved incidents stuck in there waiting to be healed?
5. Invite healing angels to come to heal your heart and sense how many come to help you.
6. Allow them to soothe, mend or heal your heart in whatever way they wish to.
7. Let them take out your heart and carry it up to a beautiful cascade. As they hold your heart in the water, sense and watch the old hurts wash away.
8. The angels are carrying your heart up to Source now for a blessing. Relax and be receptive and open to anything that may happen.
9. Send thanks for anything you have received.
10. Open up to allow your purified and blessed heart to be returned into your body.
11. Sense the angels stroking your aura, so that you are closed down and safe.
12. When you are ready, open your eyes and focus on loving thoughts.

EXERCISE: *To meet the Lords of Karma*

The Lords of Karma help us to make our life choices. They keep the akashic records, which are our balance sheets of good and bad. They will give us help and guidance if we ask for it. If you have a challenge in your life about which you wish to ask for guidance, you may like to decide on a question before you start your journey.

1. Take several deep breaths and as you release them, say 'peace' to yourself.
2. Starting with your toes, relax your body all the way to your crown.
3. Invite your angel to come close and sense or watch it coming to you. Take a moment to greet it lovingly.

4. Ask it to conduct you up to the Lords of Karma for help and guidance.
5. Let it take you by the hand and draw you up through the clouds, the stars and through the universe.
6. Breathe in light and breathe out jealousy, anger, guilt, hurt or fear. Take your time doing this.
7. Ahead of you is a beautiful white temple. Let your angel take you up the white steps and across the courtyard to the door of the room where the Lords of Karma are seated.
8. Knock and ask permission to enter. Then approach the Lords of Karma humbly and calmly.
9. Ask your question or ask for guidance to help you release karma.
10. Await a response. Even if nothing appears to happen, your request will have been noted and guidance will come as soon as you are ready to receive it.
11. Thank the Lords of Karma for admitting you and allow your angel to bring you back down to Earth.
12. Thank your angel and rest quietly before opening your eyes.

EXERCISE: *To bring spiritual qualities into your life*

In the Age of Aquarius, the new golden age, which we have just entered, we will live at a more spiritual level of consciousness. Instead of focusing on the material world, it will be our joy and delight to increase divine qualities in our lives. These may be freedom, peace, love, enthusiasm, gratitude, balance, beauty or any number of wonderful qualities which make us feel good.

One way to start this process is to invite the angels to increase in our lives the qualities we wish to focus on. This exercise will draw the angels close to you to help you do this.

1. Sit quietly and calmly. Breathe in light and breathe out love until you feel relaxed and still.
2. Decide on one or two spiritual qualities you would like to increase in your life.
3. Invite in your guardian angel and feel it enfold and support you.
4. For a few moments think of one of the qualities you wish to have more of.
5. Invite in the angel of that quality. You may see or have an impression of

this angel, its colour, its size, the way it is dressed.
6. Ask the angel to bring more of this quality into your life.
7. See, sense, feel your life filled with this higher quality.
8. Expect more of this quality to come to you.
9. Open your eyes.

EXERCISE: *To release fears*

Angels are willing and ready to help us to let go of old fears if we will only relax and trust them to do so.

1. Relax and breathe calmly and evenly.
2. Invite an angel in to help you release your fear and the tension it causes in your body.
3. You may like to think about your fear or simply breathe into the tense part of your body where you hold the fear.
4. Allow a picture, memory or symbol to float into your mind.
5. Relax while the angel or angels pull the picture, memory or symbol from you. Allow them to dissolve the fear in light.
6. They will now show you a positive picture or symbol which will help you to feel strong.
7. They are placing this symbol either into your third eye or into the part of your body which was tense.
8. Thank your angels and open your eyes.

EXERCISE: *To increase self-worth and confidence*

Our solar plexus is the seat of our lower will. It is here that we hold our sense of self-worth and confidence. Many people hold fear here. The angels are willing to help you release this now to enhance your confidence and sense of value.

1. Relax and be still.
2. Breathe into your solar plexus with long, slow, deep, even breaths.
3. Imagine you are going into your solar plexus and finding a cellar or a room. What is it like?
4. Invite your angel to take out any old memories, fears or negativities.

5. Allow your angel to pull out any darkness or dirt or dust.
6. Be aware of your angel making you a golden ball of light and filling it with confidence, worth and power.
7. Be receptive as it places this golden ball of energy into your solar plexus.
8. Breathe into it and feel your value and worth increasing.
9. Thank your angel and open your eyes.

EXERCISE: *Freedom from attachment*

We cannot enjoy anything if we are attached to it because we fear we will be unhappy if we lose it. This applies to material possessions, hobbies, jobs and sometimes even qualities such as anger. So in the new consciousness it is fine to have things as long as we are clear our ego does not need them.

It is the same with people. Need of any description forms cords which attach us to others and cause us to manipulate them emotionally and also allow ourselves to be manipulated. Unconditional love forms no cords and leaves people totally free to be themselves.

The angels are willing to help us release, uncord and set ourselves and others free.

1. Let your whole body relax and become comfortable and at ease.
2. Decide what or who you are now ready to release.
3. See or sense it or them in front of you.
4. Be aware of whatever links you to it.
5. Invite an angel in to sever the link and dissolve the cords right to the roots. Be aware you may feel this in your physical body.
6. Ask the angel to fill you with a higher quality to help you let this go from your life.
7. Breathe in the higher quality.
8. Thank the angel and open your eyes.

EXERCISE: *To heal your inner child*

Most of us have an inner child who is stuck or lost and hurting. Whenever we have pain in our body we can be sure that our inner child is telling us that it is in pain and causing disruption in our energy flow.

When we feel hurt, frightened, angry, jealous, envious, obstinate or not good enough, there is a part of us still stuck in childhood, creating problems in our life. The angels are very happy to help us heal these stuck parts of ourselves if we ask them to.

1. Take a few moments to loosen the joints of your body and relax.
2. Breathe comfortably into your tummy, expanding it, and then slowly release the breath. Repeat this several times until you begin to feel very comfortable.
3. Remember the last time you felt angry, hurt or negative in any way. Be aware that the balanced wise adult is not feeling these emotions. The emotions are those of your stuck child. Sense how old is this child within you.
4. When you find the child, comfort it and invite in the healing angels to heal it.
5. Relax and be open to whatever the angels do to heal the child.
6. When they return your child to you notice how different it looks and feels.
7. Thank the angels.
8. Hold and love your inner child.

EXERCISE: *To heal your ancestors*

So much pain and hurt is passed down through generations. So many unresolved family patterns continue along the line. These are the issues which keep too many souls stuck in the heavy energy field around planet Earth causing them to reincarnate again and again. Angels are ready and willing to help us release ourselves and our ancestors.

1. Breathe down into your feet until they feel heavy and comfortable. Then breathe down into your legs until they too feel very relaxed. Do the same with your hands, your arms, your back and your trunk.
2. Invite the appropriate angels to come to you and relax in their wonderful energy.
3. Explain to the angels what the pattern is you need help with.
4. Have a sense of the line of ancestors all carrying the burden of this pattern.
5. Allow the angels to lift you up through the universe, higher and higher until you can see a radiant white light. Within this light is Source.

6. With the angels, kneel and ask for grace for yourself and your ancestors.
7. A symbol will be given to you if grace is granted.
8. Return down to Earth with the symbol and pass it back along the line of ancestors.
9. Thank the angels and open your eyes.

EXERCISE: *Sending Angel Blessings*

People only behave badly because they are hurting or don't feel worth while or confident. Decide to stop judging them. Instead start to wonder what they need to make them feel happy, then bless them with that quality. Ask the angels to work through you by sending the qualities to the other person or people in a golden light.

For example, if someone is sarcastic, they feel vulnerable and are trying to keep people away from them by sending out little sarcastic darts. Bless them with love and self worth and visualise them feeling safe, open and loving.

If someone keeps complaining they don't have any money, bless them with abundance – and picture them being showered with plenty. When you pass a school ask the angels to bless the children with confidence, happiness and the ability to absorb lessons easily. You might like to ask them to bless the teachers with patience and love of teaching.

When you do the blessing game remember that everything you send to others comes back to you.

1. Sit quietly in a comfortable place or you can do this while walking or driving.
2. If you are visualising this, close your eyes and take a deep centring breath. Otherwise keep your eyes open!
3. Picture a person, situation or place that needs help.
4. Decide what qualities that person, situation or place needs in order to make them feel happy, light and whole.
5. Ask the angels to come to you, and you may be surprised at how many enter your inner world.
6. Ask the angels to send a golden blessing of the qualities you decide are needed, to the person, situation or place you have been thinking of.
7. Visualise or sense the energy going to and surrounding its destination.

8. Imagine everything whole and perfect there.
9. Thank the angels.
10. Open yourself up to receiving blessings in your turn and visualise wonderful things coming to you.

EXERCISE: *Be a magnet for good things*

Every thought and emotion you have creates your energy and this acts like a magnet to bring people and situations into your life. Each thought and emotion has a colour. For example, if someone is sad and depleted their aura may become grey, which draws in loneliness and unhappiness. If you are sociable and friendly your colours may be warm orange, which will attract in similar warm, sociable and friendly people into your life.

If you want to have a happy, love filled, successful or abundant life, this visualisation and exercise will enable the angels to work with you to create what you desire.

- First decide what you want to have more of in your life.
- If you want to spend more time in nature use green.
- For more fun and happiness use orange with red in it.
- For more wise, quiet, peaceful, centred friends use gold.
- For more angelic connection use gold.
- For the ability to study and pass exams use yellow.
- For more healing ability use blue or green.
- For more love use pink.
- For courage use deep blue.

For confidence and happiness use a golden orange. This is the example we are going to use in the exercise below, but you can change the colour according to your needs, so before you start decide what qualities you want to attract and the colour you will use. While it is wonderful if you can visualise it, just focussing on it, will fill your aura with this colour in a way that will impact on your own feelings and that of others.

1. Sit quietly and relax.
2. With each in breath imagine you are breathing in a wonderful golden orange colour. Take as long as you wish to breathe each one into every part of your body.

3. With each out breath, picture a golden orange glow filling your aura.
4. Then sit in your golden orange light for a few minutes visualising your confident, happy aura reaching out and touching people.
5. Ask the angels to come in and touch your aura with happy sparkles.
6. Visualise yourself going out into the life you want, with this aura round you. It is full of sparkling light and the angels are with you.
7. Be aware how people are responding to you.
8. Notice how situations change.
9. Feel the energy of places lightening up. Know that you can breathe this colour round you whenever you need to and the angels will add extra light.
10. Relax for a few moments knowing you can magnetise the life you want.

EXERCISE: *Be strong and courageous*

If you have difficult situations or people to face you will need extra strength and courage, so ask Archangel Michael to help you. He carries a Sword of Truth and a Shield of Protection. He also puts a deep blue cloak of protection round you.

Whether you need courage to face the dentist, travel on a journey, talk to your boss or partner or take on a new business, he will assist. At any time you can call him in and he will come. But if you want to do a deeper visualisation, the following will bring his energy more deeply into you.

1. Sit quietly where you will not be disturbed.
2. Breathe comfortably until you feel relaxed.
3. Think or say aloud, 'Archangel Michael, please come and help me now.'
4. Visualise him placing a deep blue protective cloak round you. Picture it being zipped up from your feet to your throat and the hood placed over your head and pulled down over your third eye. Take time to make sure it is fully in place.
5. Imagine other people's comments or challenges bouncing off the protection, like arrows against a wall.
6. Then Archangel Michael places his Sword of Truth in your right hand and his Shield of Protection in your left. He is standing beside you and you feel like a powerful warrior. You can face anybody or anything.

7. You are filled with calmness and confidence. Nothing and no one can bother or harm you. Archangel Michael is beside you.
8. Imagine you are dealing with the difficult person or situation in a calm, centred and empowered way.
9. See a positive outcome for the highest good of all.
10. Feel the great feeling of handling this so courageously and confidently.
11. Thank Archangel Michael for his help.
12. Then open your eyes, knowing that you can ask Archangel Michael for help as often as you need to.

EXERCISE: *Heart rose*

When your heart is warm and loving, you have many friends and happy relationships. Your empathy and compassion enable you to become very psychic and to help and heal people. You feel genuinely loved. Here is a very simple and beautiful visualisation you can do with Archangel Chamuel, the angel of love.

1. Find a place where you can be quiet
2. Gently rub your heart centre, in the middle of your chest.
3. Spend a few moments thinking about all your blessings and the good things in your life.
4. Then acknowledge all your gifts and good qualities.
5. Ask Archangel Chamuel to touch your heart and you may sense or feel this.
6. Visualise a velvety pink rose in the centre of your chest.
7. Archangel Chamuel is opening out the beautiful petals one by one.
8. You may sense his energy moving over your heart, until the rose is fully open.
9. Imagine the golden sun shining down on the rose in your heart, filling it with warmth and light.
10. Archangel Chamuel is blessing your rose, which is releasing a wonderful fragrance.
11. Be aware of a pink light flowing from your heart to people, situations and places.
12. Be aware of love from others coming to you. Let it enter your heart.
13. Imagine your relationships when your heart rose is radiating love.
14. Notice how safe people feel with you.

15. When you have fully experienced your heart open, decide whether or not you want to leave it open or close it a little.
16. Thank Archangel Chamuel.
17. Remember your heart centre will become more beautiful each time you do this visualisation.

EXERCISE: *Decisions pathways*

If you are not quite sure which decision to make Archangel Gabriel brings clarity and helps to purify the energy, so that you can move forward. It may help to write down your options. This may enable you to eliminate some possibilities until you have two choices left.

1. Sit quietly and comfortably where you won't be disturbed.
2. Close your eyes and let yourself relax.
3. Imagine you are standing at a crossroads and think about the choices you have in front of you.
4. There are two possible paths ahead.
5. Ask Archangel Gabriel in his pure white light to stand beside you to help you make the highest possible decision.
6. Walk with Archangel Gabriel down the first path and experience exactly what it feels like if you make this choice.
7. Then do the same with the second one.
8. When you return to the crossroads you may have made a decision from your heart.
9. If you have not, ask Archangel Gabriel to give you a sign now or at some later time in the day.
10. Thank him for his help.
11. Open your eyes, knowing that you being guided to the right decision.

May angels fill you

with an abundance of love,

peace, joy and success so that

your heart overflows

with happiness.

Angels Of Light Cards

BY

Diana Cooper

Angels are waiting and happy to help you at all times. Under Spiritual Law they cannot step in until you ask. Whenever you have a problem, there is an angel standing by you, awaiting your permission to assist.

Angels cannot and will not help you if you ask for something from neediness and greed. Nor will they help you receive something which is not spiritually right. Recognise your authority and make your requests from wisdom and strength. You may also ask the angels to help someone else for his or her highest good, not necessarily for what you think that highest good might be. Your thoughts to that person create a rainbow bridge along which the angels can travel to help him or her.

You can also ask the angels to help the planet.

Each of the 52 Angel Cards included in this deck represent a different Angel quality, and can be used for guidance, inspiration and affirmation. The cards will help you tune in to the higher vibrations of the Angels, and allow you to feel the helping hands of these beings at all times. Following the inspiration of the Angels will raise your consciousness, which will automatically help you attract to yourself people and situations of a higher vibratory level and release old negative thought patterns. Carry these cards with you wherever you go and use them to remind yourself of the presence, guidance and help of the Angels in your life, always and everywhere. You are never alone or lost when the Angels are with you.

Set of 52 cards + 2 instructions cards
in desktop presentation stand with slipcase – ISBN 978-1-84409-141-6
***Pocket edition:** set of 52 cards + 2 instructions cards*
in tuckbox – ISBN 978-1-84409-171-3

FINDHORN PRESS

Books, Card Sets,
CDs & DVDs
that inspire and uplift

For a complete catalogue,
please contact:

Findhorn Press Ltd
305a The Park, Findhorn
Forres IV36 3TE
Scotland, UK

Telephone
+44-(0)1309-690582
Fax
+44-(0)131-777-2711
eMail
info@findhornpress.com

or consult our catalogue online
(with secure order facility) on
www.findhornpress.com

For information on the Findhorn Foundation:
www.findhorn.org